Can God Use Me— At This Age?

As you look at all the needs in the world around you, you might be saying, "What on earth can I do? Any help I give would be like trying to drain the sea with a bucket."

Eveline Ritchie felt the same way. Until she decided that all God wanted was for her to do her part—to take out her bucketful.

The result has been a "retirement" more exciting than she had ever imagined. Let her amazing story show you how the senior years can be the greatest of your life!

Taking Out My Bucketful

Eveline Ritchie
with Violet T. Pearson

To God be the glory
Eveline Ritchie

ACCENT BOOKS
Denver, Colorado

MEMBER OF
EVANGELICAL CHRISTIAN
PUBLISHERS ASSOCIATION

COVER: The author is shown with the young sons of Dr. and Mrs. Yun Chung Sun of Midland, Michigan. Mrs. Sun interested Miss Ritchie in Taiwan.

ACCENT BOOKS
A division of Accent-B/P Publications
12100 W. Sixth Avenue
P.O. Box 15337
Denver, Colorado 80215

Copyright © 1978 Accent-B/P Publications
Printed in the United States of America

Library of Congress Catalog Card Number: 78-67935

ISBN 0-89636-009-1

Dedication

Dedicated to retirees or about-to-be retired
everywhere, especially to those who find
the later years of life boring and a burden,
instead of full of joy and exciting
new opportunities.

Acknowledgment

Grateful acknowledgment is made to:

Interested friends who encouraged me to have my experiences published;

Pastor Mark Dickerson and Mrs. Frank Justice for reviewing the trial manuscript for criticism;

Mr. Torrey Barcanic from Moody Bible Institute who especially urged me in this endeavor and gave helpful suggestions;

Violet T. Pearson of Accent Books for offering her professional skill in preparing the manuscript for publication.

In appreciation of your prayers and friendship —

Contents

CHAPTER 1

Getting My Bucket

RETIREMENT! I don't even like the word. It sounds so final, like everything in life is over. It smells like mothballs. Something taken out of circulation and put away on a shelf. Even Mr. Webster says that retirement is withdrawing from public life, solitude, retreating, and seclusion.

Not a very exciting future.

What thoughts fill *your* mind as you contemplate your sunset years? Do you look forward to them with apprehension, dreading the thought of loneliness and nothing to do? Or with anticipation of days filled with joyful living—and the time to do it in?

It is possible for these years to be the most exciting time of your life. They have been for me. I have had experiences I never dreamed would be mine.

There is no place in the life of a Christian for retirement in the sense of sitting around doing nothing. Busy people are generally the happiest. To have interesting work to do and an aim in life is very good therapy for the body as well as the mind and soul. The Bible says, "They [the righteous] shall still bring forth fruit in old age; they shall be fat and flourishing" (Psalms 92:14). God expects us to be busy as long as we live. He says, "Occupy till I come" (Luke 19:13).

God has a definite plan for every life that continues as long as that life lasts. He can use older people in many areas where younger ones lack maturity, understanding and experience. There are also many ways in which people can serve even with handicaps. I have read about people who were bedfast and paralyzed for years, and when friends came to cheer them up they went away comforted themselves.

Everyone has a talent in some way, and it should be allowed to function as long as possible. The older segment of our population is a gold mine of resources and skills waiting to be tapped. What a waste of skills and abilities that have been developed over a lifetime if we allow them to fall into disuse—just because somebody says we are not capable of working after we have reached a certain age!

So often we are just ready to count for the most when we are forced to retire. Some of the greatest music, art, literature, inventions and discoveries have been produced by people who were in their later years. How I wish I had known as much about teaching when I began as I did when I closed my classroom door for the last time! How much better a job I could have done.

As long as God allows us to live, there is work for us to do. We have only one life to contribute to humanity and we should give it our best as long as possible. Remember, "Only what's done for Christ will last."

Many people feel that when they reach this time of life they are too old to begin anything new. That is where they are very wrong. We have so much going for us during these years. We have a freedom of life not experienced before. We have left behind the frustration of making a living. We can set our goals and if we fail to reach them, we do not have to fear we will lose our jobs. We do not have to work when we do not feel able. Since we are no longer on the job market, we can make a job for ourselves to suit our needs and abilities.

Do you wonder what you can do? Just ask God to direct you. He has all kinds of jobs, something that will be just right for everyone. He has a work for you that no one else can do.

My hobbies, like weaving and sewing, opened up a whole new life for me.

There is so much to be done. The tremendous needs of this old world are staggering in comparison with what a single individual would be capable of doing to help. We must remember that God does not require that all needs be met by one person. Mrs. Lillian Dixon, who has become a legend in Taiwan for the great humanitarian work she is doing, was told by an official that some project she was planning was like trying to drain the sea with a bucket. She replied that since she was a Christian, she must take out her bucketful.

That thought made a tremendous impact upon my

life. Really, all that God asks of us is that we each do our bit—take out our own bucketful. Buckets come in many sizes. Some can hold a large amount while others are small. God only asks us to fill the size He gives to us. No life is too small for God to use, nor too insignificant to have an influence for either good or bad. He knows how to tailor a job to suit the person, and He will supply all that is needed to get the job done. He has done it for me.

My hobbies of many years have opened up a whole new life for me in my sunset years. Because of skills developed through my hobbies, I have had a wonderful time extending my horizons, cultivating new friendships both here and in faraway places, developing new activities, and experiencing the most thrilling adventures one can imagine. My hobbies have served as my "bucket."

What are your interests? Your hobbies? Your developed skills? Consider! How could God use them to make your golden years truly fulfilling? Commit them to Him for His service—and see what God can do. Who knows? You, too, may find your retirement years to be the happiest time of your life!

CHAPTER 2

Dipping In

I will never forget that momentous afternoon in early June, 1961. I was sitting in my empty classroom in Midland, Michigan, silently watching the hands of the clock on the wall make their way to the hour of three. At that time I would terminate forever my thirty-six years as a public school teacher, most of them spent teaching second and third graders.

Many happy memories passed through my mind. Problems that almost defied solution also crowded in. The growing tensions and pressures of the teaching profession were taking their toll with my nerves. My patience was becoming so thin I could see through it in places. I felt it was time to turn the reins over to younger hands.

I had loved teaching. You might say I came from a family of teachers. My father was a country school teacher, and my mother taught a few terms before her marriage. My younger brother also did a bit of teaching. As a teacher I did my best to make school life interesting and worthwhile for my pupils. Now, after all these years, I wanted to do something different while I was still physically able.

So this was the day that would usher in a new era for me. For years I had looked forward to the day when I would be 62 years old and could spend unlimited time doing the many interesting hobbies and projects I had planned.

Through the years I had developed many skills. As a teenager I never craved to be on the go all the time. Instead, I came to have a great interest in creative hobbies. There were my oil and water color painting, metal tooling, many kinds of fancy work, handloom weaving, stamp collecting. I had studied a half dozen musical instruments. And there was my newest hobby—the raising of African violets. Now I looked forward to a variety of things to do. I had quite a program of self-gratification planned for my coming days.

I began to enjoy my new freedom.

Then one day the thought really struck me hard: "Eveline, you have planned a very selfish life for yourself!"

The activities in themselves were above reproach, of course. But I had given little thought or planning for special service for the Lord and others. I was allowing hobbies to become my master instead of my servants.

My parents were Christians, so I had the benefit of being raised in a Christian home. I accepted Jesus Christ as my personal Saviour when I was in my early teens. Attending church was a regular habit through the years. I have served in a number of capacities in the church, especially in the line of music. Concern for the unfortunate, especially lepers, began early in my life. It has continued and extended to include orphans and all in need. But I cannot recall that I had ever included in my planning for the future the idea of asking God to direct my planning.

I seriously faced the fact that someday I would have to stand before God and give an account to Him of how I had spent my time, my talents, and my money. The Bible says, "Every man's work shall be made manifest: for the day shall declare it, because it shall be revealed by fire; and the fire shall try every man's work of what sort it is" (I Corinthians 3:13). I wanted to accomplish something that would stand the test of fire.

I told God I was turning my life over to Him completely. I asked Him to direct my life and give me something to do that would honor Him and be a blessing to the world. Home responsibilities with my elderly father required that what I would do had to be done at home. I couldn't get away. So God took me at my word and brought the world to my door!

Some five years before I retired, I had learned about the terrible conditions in Greece following World War II. There were many thousands of orphan children just roaming the streets with no one to care. The American Mission to Greeks was trying desperately to help these children through orphanages. This organization had been doing a tremendous amount of good for the poor in Greece and was now extending its ministry in India and other countries with its Newspaper Evangelism and humanitarian work. Clothing was greatly needed for the war orphans.

My heart was touched. Countless numbers of orphans have seen more trouble in their short lives than the most of us will encounter in a lifetime. Millions today are suffering from illness, starvation, desertion, loneliness, and no one to care whether they live or die—little souls for whom Christ died! I knew they were very dear to the heart of God because so many "fatherless" are mentioned in the Bible. They have a right to the good things in life as much as do children who have parents to care for their needs.

With this burden on my heart, I felt that perhaps I could find some time in spite of my teaching duties and responsibilities at home to make a few garments for the war orphans in Greece. I wrote to see if new clothing was acceptable, as many times the duty on new clothing is prohibitive.

One afternoon as I came home from school there was a letter for me accepting my offer. I could scarcely wait for the next afternoon to come so I could go to the J. C. Penney store and look through their box of remnants for materials.

I will never forget that evening. Mother told me to get at my sewing and she would take care of the supper work. What a joy it was to feel I was actually doing something to supply a need! Many days at school I would work through the noon hour with a sandwich in one hand and a pencil in the other, correcting papers or making lesson plans so I would have some extra time in the evening to sew for the orphans.

I made several shipments to an orphanage in Katerini, Greece. Mr. and Mrs. Mark Diavastes were in charge, and they sent me pictures of little girls dressed in the clothing I had made. To see their sweet faces brought tears to my eyes.

I made clothing for a children's rescue home, a leper colony, a baby hospital, and other orphanages in Greece. By the time I quit teaching I had made about 200 garments. I can see now how God was getting me ready for my new job after "retirement."

My mother passed away in 1958, which left me with all the housework to do and an ailing father to care for—in addition to my teaching duties. This did not leave me much time for sewing. After I quit teaching in 1961, my father's health was failing considerably and during the last five years of his life I had the entire care of him. I was away from home only one night during that time.

In the fall after I was free from school duties, and after I had asked God to direct my life and give me

It brought tears to my eyes to see the sweet faces of the orphans in Greece who were wearing the dresses I had made. (I did not make the dress marked "X.")

something to do that would honor Him and be a blessing to the world, I saw an advertisement in a religious magazine. It showed a number of pictures of sad-faced little Korean orphans. They looked as though they had never smiled. An appeal was made for sponsors by the organization then known as the Everett Swanson Evangelistic Association, now named Compassion, which has orphanages in many countries.

For many years I had had a strange feeling about the Orient. The very word "Orient" sounded mystical and exciting to me, and the appeal in the Compassion advertisement gave me a strong desire to sponsor an orphan in the Orient. So I answered the appeal. The organization sent me a sheet of paper with the pictures of twelve children on it for me to choose one. What a difficult job that was! Each child's face seemed to plead, "Please take me."

I could take only one. I finally decided on a girl, twelve-year-old Kim Yung Sook. (Kim is her family name and Yung Sook her given name.) I wanted a child old enough to write to me, because adults have to write for the small ones. I wanted to have a personal communication with my adopted child in the Orient.

It was such a joy to exchange letters and pictures with Yung Sook. She was almost overcome with joy when she learned she had an "American Mother." She had felt sad because one of her sisters, who was also at the orphanage, had a sponsor and she didn't. It gave me a wonderful feeling to be able to bring so much happiness to the heart of a child.

Of course, I wanted to make some dresses for Yung Sook, but I didn't know what size would fit her. So I thought of a solution. I made ten dresses of several sizes and pinned a number on each and kept a record of the size of each number. Then I asked her to tell me which number fit her. That way I would learn her size and the rest of the clothing could be given to other girls.

Yung Sook wrote me in Korean and an interpreter translated it and sent me the English version. "You have no idea how happy I am whenever I receive your letter," she wrote. "I really feel the love you send across the many thousand miles to me. How I wish I could meet you and talk to you in person, but all I can do is think of you and keep praying for you. I always remember you in my prayer."

It meant so much to me that my little Korean child was praying for me! Her letter continued, "Thank you very much for the wonderful package I received from you. When I got your package I danced with joy. Other friends envy me very much. I am at a loss how to thank you for your wonderful gifts. I was very excited when I opened your package and saw so many lovely gifts you sent me."

That experience gave me another exciting idea. I would make clothing for children who had no sponsors. I have read that such children often cry themselves to sleep when a sponsored child receives a gift from his or her sponsor and they never get anything. I sent quite a few boxes of clothing to be given to unsponsored children.

A group of dresses ready to be sent to an orphanage in Korea. No two are alike.

I wanted to send gifts to Yung Sook but I didn't want the other children to feel jealous of her. So I always sent extra things she could share with her friends. There was such a note of pride in her letters when she told me how she had shared the gifts with others.

These children can never learn the joy of sharing if they have nothing to share. It always made me feel so sad when she would tell me how others envied her having a "mother" in America. That told me volumes about how lonely they were for attention and for someone to love them. So many are still hoping and praying that someone will care enough to be their sponsor.

Yung Sook was learning to play the piano, so I sent her several music books. She was also interested in collecting stamps. I sent her a stamp album and packages of stamps. I learned a few years later that the stamp album had become a treasure of the orphanage and was displayed for visitors to see. How deeply they appreciate the smallest attention! I sent a pretty greeting card to one child who prized it so deeply she said she was going to keep it forever.

I was so involved with my little Korean daughter that I thought my own personal cup—or was it my bucket?—was full and running over with happiness. But God had more blessings in store for me in the days ahead.

CHAPTER 3

My Bucket Runneth Over

The following spring I saw some more pictures of Korean orphans and again felt a tug at my heart. I had tasted the joy of being a sponsor with lovely Kim Yung Sook and was hungry for more.

I consulted my budget and, although it wasn't as strong as it was while I was teaching, I decided to apply for another orphan, even if I had to do some sacrificing to see it through. Looking back on those days now, I don't remember that any real sacrificing was ever necessary. If there was, I didn't realize it because of the joy I was experiencing.

There was also a great need for sponsors to support native pastors. I thought it would be wonderful to have a pastor representing me on the foreign field. I decided to sponsor both another orphan and a pastor. Little Shim Soon Ja and pastor Wi Myung Ib joined my growing family.

Since Soon Ja's mother was a leper, the child was in a home for the children of leper parents. She was so happy to have a sponsor. I told her how much I would love to put my arms around her. She answered that her own mother had never said that. How very deeply their hearts crave to be loved.

Soon Ja wrote to me from Korea, "Dearest Mommy, I want to thank you very, very much for your Christmas package. I was so thrilled and so excited to get it. I jumped for joy to see the nice doll on the bed. I have never seen such a pretty doll. It looks very, very pretty. My friends envy me so much. Thank you so much for it. I like it so very much. I do wish you could visit our country. I am praying to God for making this possible for me to see you even once."

Shim Soon Ja became my second sponsored child.

The doll I had sent to Soon Ja was a good-size one which required a large shipping box, and I used clothing for packing. Soon Ja wrote that it was the largest box any child had received and all the children were jealous of her and she was so proud of it. Oh, my! Proud of others being jealous of her! Then I thought, no one was ever jealous of her rags, her hungry stomach or having a leper mother. To have something so desirable that the others wished they had it was almost too much for her little heart to contain. She has now become of age and has left the orphanage to do sewing and commercial knitting, for which she was trained.

Since my heart has gone out to unfortunate lepers for years, I wanted to make clothing for more of the children of leper parents. So I wrote Compassion for the address of one of this kind of orphanages under their supervision. I then sent a letter to the superintendent, Rev. Bae Sun Kung, to tell him that a box of new clothing was on the way to the orphanage.

Pastor Bae later told me that he was so overjoyed at the prospect of the clothing he called his staff together and they had a praise service to thank God. He told me they rarely received new clothing. I continued to send clothing to this orphanage for a number of years.

Later, Pastor Bae was given a responsible denominational position and his wife, Jo Jum Si, took his place as superintendent. In Korea the family name comes first, as I have mentioned, and the second and third names are spoken together as a first name. Instead of saying "Reverend Kung," as we would be apt to, it should be "Reverend Bae." Women do not take their husband's name when they marry. Rev. Bae's wife wrote me one time, asking if I would be her big sister. That made me very happy. She has been such a dear friend.

Several years later, one of Yung Sook's sisters found her at the orphanage and took her to her home to live and go to school. So my sponsorship for her was ended. I had a good idea of what the feeling is like for parents when a child leaves home. In most cases the parents can see the child again, or receive letters, but for me it was the end of a precious relationship. Since no provision is made for

translation of letters after a child leaves an
orphanage, it is too difficult to keep track of them. I
felt just lost for a time.

Yung Sook's superintendent and I had become
good friends, however, through the translation of
our letters. Whenever she saw Yung Sook, she would
tell me anything of interest about her. I was told that
Yung Sook married an air force pilot and I haven't
heard anything more about her for a long time.

When a sponsored child leaves an orphanage, the
picture of another child needing a sponsor is
submitted to the former sponsor for approval. Baek
Kyung Ill, a very pitiful and undernourished little
boy was assigned to me in Yung Sook's place. The
child was so happy to have a "Mommy." His letters
were precious. Here is one: "I feel to myself you
answer to my call when I call you Mommy in a soft
voice. I have received your nice picture and loving
letter. When I see you in the picture, I long to come
into your bosom. How happy I shall be when I have a
time to meet you in the face and am taken pictures
along with you in the picture.

"You said you are now at the age of 68. Our
superintendent is also woman and aged 64. I have
been proud of you who still works regardless of your
age, and think of me as your child. I pray that God
may bless you with the best of your health."

Little Kyung Ill disappeared from the orphanage
several months later and was never found. I have
heard that relatives sometimes slip into the orphanage and steal children back because of their
embarrassment in having to abandon them.

During the Korean war many thousands of
children were left homeless and often both parents
were killed. Members of families were scattered and
it would be years before they would find each other—
if they were lucky. Many never did. In later times,

dire poverty has caused abandonment of children and they finally are rescued and placed in orphanages. Sometimes relatives find the children and take them into their homes to live.

This is what happened to the next child I sponsored. Kim Kil Hwan was a brilliant student, but he was found by his uncle and, according to Korean law, the orphanage had to let him go. He loved so much to write to "Mommy."

Kim Kil Hwan shows the Christmas gifts he bought with the gift money I sent him.

"I am so happy," he wrote one time, "to stay under the love of God and am so happy to know you as my sponsor. I am now in 11 years old and in 3 grade of Primary school. 106 children in our Home go to school. We go to school at 8 o'clock A.M. and come back at 1 o'clock P.M. We learn Korean language, mathematics, social life, physical education, picture drawing, and music. We usually study 4 hours a days. We have 113 boys and 43 girls in our Home and have family worship services and midweek night. And we also study Bible. I will pray for you. Please remember me in your prayer.

"Thank you very much for your $3 Christmas gift. I bought 2 towels, 5 notebooks, 1 dozen pencils, 1 crayon, 1 toy, 1 great men's book, and 2 packages of candy with the money. How did you spend your Christmas day? We had a celebrating worship on Christmas eve and also had chorus, duet, drama, contest against each team. Those who played well received a wonderful prize. I will pray for you."

Yoon Chook Hyun said he would like to call me his dear Grandmother and would pray for me.

It was quite different in the case of Yoon Chook Hyun. He had three brothers and sisters at the orphanage and his mother was given work there so she could be with her family. He was such a friendly boy, with an outgoing personality, which showed in

28

his letters.

Chook Hyun was beginning junior high school. He wrote in one letter how he was collecting stamps and already had eighty stamps. I sent money to Compassion for a stamp album for him and they promised to see that he would get packets of stamps which I enclosed in my letters.

From some of the comments in his letters he must have almost gone wild when one of my letters arrived. He took his album to school and his teacher had him place it on display for others to see, which made him very happy. He told me that when he got lonesome he would look at the stamps and think of me. He also said he "kissed on the stamps."

I had to tell him that wasn't very good for the stamps, but I often had to chuckle as I read his letters. In one letter he said, "I was very excited to receive the Christmas gift money of $5.00 you sent me. I bought with the money: sport shoes, lunch box, five note books, soccer ball, a dozen of lead pencils, eraser, knife, and sweet candies. Thank you very much for your kindness.

"I will be a steady junior high school boy since next year and will go to school with new sport shoes and notebooks. How much happy I was to receive your letter and pretty card and picture. I kissed ten times in the picture. I am sure you are very benevolent like Jesus Christ. We had lots of snow in our town and made the snowmen and played the snowball fight. I keep your picture on my desk to see every day. I would like to call you my dear Grandmother and pray to God for you. May God bless you."

One day I received a letter from the superintendent of this children's home saying, "Your beloved foster child left our home on last November 30. He was very disappointed when he left our home. His uncle who manages a furnishing store in Seoul took him to teach the technic. He said leaving our home that he would look at the stamps you sent when he would miss you. He said also that he would be a fine man to reward for your love and would pray to God for your kindness given him during that time. You are always in our thought and prayers. May God bless you always."

I am going to miss this lad's letters the most of any boy I have sponsored. I always wonder when they leave the Home, with its Christian influence, if they will have Christian training and have love and kindness shown to them. As they are not able to write in English, it isn't possible to keep in touch with them. One has to just leave them with the Lord to look after them. It is such a joy to have a few years to show them love and a concern for their welfare. I thank God for the opportunity He has given to bring a little sunshine into darkened lives. How I hope to meet every one of them in Heaven someday!

Little eight-year-old Yoo Jae Hwak, whom I am now sponsoring is such a sad looking child, living in a poverty-stricken home. He is in a family-helper project which helps the child in the home. A pastor wrote for him and said he was so happy to have a sponsor. Compassion tries to keep children in family atmospheres when possible so they will grow up more naturally. The attitude toward orphans is changing in Korea today and more people are adopting the homeless.

I have sponsored five native pastors. All of them worked under great difficulties, as some of the excerpts from their letters will tell.

"Greetings to you in the name of our Lord. I pray that God's amazing grace be with you as you do His will. It is a great joy for me to have a sponsor in America, for this means there is a person who helps me spiritually and materially as I serve this church. I have been a Christian these ten years and trained at seminary for five years. I believe God called me to this ministry. The village was like wilderness that the Christians in the church were calling for a preacher. This made me think for what God has called me to this village. The building is built with clay and bricks on 19 Pyung of land. The church cannot support itself now. They helped former preacher only one tenth of what he needed. We had Vacation Bible School in August and there met nearly one hundred children. We have new converts this month and they are coming to church regularly as others. May God bless you."

* * *

"Many thanks for your support. If you did not help me, I might starve now, my church would be indebted, my rooms would not be warm and Christians would be thought ill of, for the unbelievers would say, 'Why Lee Yo Sup has nothing to eat, and why his rooms are cold?' Because you help me both materially and spiritually, our God is being glorified."

* * *

"I am very sorry that our church bell was stolen during the month of August. While I was leading the family service of our church members in the evening it was stolen. It is a very sad thing to our church, because most of our believers live far away and have no watch. In these circumstances we are faced by a great trouble in starting our meetings every day."

* * *

"This is the second Christmas for our church. We were so happy and grateful to have our new church this year. Our new church is not completed yet. My

31

church still roofed with tent canvas. It is supported by board. The ground is covered with straw sacks instead of the floor. Even the weather was so cold around Christmas, we bought a small stove in our church and it kept us warm. God has been so good for us."

* * *

Speaking of his converts, Ki Poong says, "They are willing to memorialize our church for our Lord's name and Eveline Ritchie, who is mother in the Lord. All of us will never forget your kindness for us in the Lord. They would like to devote themselves for evangelizing Word and relief work in the Lord like you. We would like to have our new church for memorializing your faithfulness and your name, then we can be glorified to our God.

"And then we are going to make our church as a model church in Korea. We are doing our best for that. We are praying for that. We hanged your picture which was sent by you on the wall of our church. All of the church members like your picture very much. Everyone says that you are the mother in the Lord. I thank you for your praying for me. I shall never forget your kindness, your prayers, your tears, your material aid to me."

I believe all these pastors tried to reach the lost. There are still many idol worshipers in their land and they often made trouble for the Christian pastors.

Each month the pastors I supported sent a report of the attendance at all services, number of homes visited, tracts distributed, number of converts, and the amount of the rice collection. Other pertinent items of interest were included. They tried to make me feel that, because I supported them so they could give their time for evangelism, I shared equally in the soul harvest. What a precious thought!

The fourth pastor, Lee Yo Sup, was the most aggressive. He tried so hard to get an industry going to give people work as so many were very poor. They tried weaving baskets to sell and wanted me to find a market for them over here, but there was too much competition in that business for an idea like that to work out. It was difficult to get some of them to see that many of their requests were not possible to fulfill. They seemed to feel that anything was possible in America. I suppose I would have felt the same had I been in their circumstances.

My name, Eveline, in the Korean language is, Ae Bool Lin, meaning, they tell me, "distributing love to neighbor." I was astonished to learn that, because that was what I was trying to do, little realizing that my name had such a beautiful meaning in their language. A pastor who knew of my work wanted his church to take that as their motto and changed the name of the church to "Eveline Church." Ki Poong's church wanted to show their appreciation for me sponsoring their pastor so changed the name of their church to "Eveline Ritchie Baptist Church."

Some of the people formed an organization to form new churches, and they named it "The Eveline Ritchie Evangelistic Association," and new churches were to be named "Eveline Churches." I was named the president, with another member acting for me over there.

It has given me a strange feeling to have churches named for me. I didn't feel I had done anything outstanding enough for such recognition. It touched me deeply, for I know there was deep Christian love back of it and a great desire to show appreciation.

Another namesake in Korea brings chuckles every time I think of it. This was another of Lee Yo Sup's brainstorms. He and a pastor friend wanted to do

I knew there was deep Christian love back of naming this Korean church for me.

something to help beggar boys to earn enough money to buy one meal a day, so they organized a business where the boys gathered up old rags and scrap paper to sell. Their center of operations was a large tent with the sign, "Eveline Ritchie Company" in large letters. Was I shocked when I learned I was in the old rag and scrap paper business!

"Timothy" Ki Poong, the last pastor I sponsored, passed away during his two-year assignment. He wasn't strong, and neither was his wife who died shortly after, leaving four little orphans. She had been in a tuberculosis sanitarium for some time.

Compassion would sponsor a pastor for two years at one location, long enough to get a church organized and self-supporting. It was interesting to note in the pastors' reports that the amount of rice collected at each service was given, along with the money offering, which was never a large amount.

Contact with the fourth orphanage I helped for

I was also honored to learn I was in the old rag and scrap paper business!

several years came to me in a different way. One day Lee Yo Sup visited a young single friend who was the superintendent of an orphanage not far from Yo Sup's home. He told Superintendent Kim Woon Suk about the work I was doing for children and pastors. Mr. Kim was deeply impressed. I guess he thought it was a "good deal for the poor people," as he later expressed it, and wanted his orphanage to get in on it.

Mr. Kim sent me a box of souvenirs which his orphans made to sell. I almost didn't get it because it was missent to a person in Wisconsin. If Mr. Kim thought his little plan would interest me in his children, it worked. I made clothing for his Home for several years.

I have a large collection of pictures showing how the children looked in clothing I sent them. These proved to me that children actually received what was sent them. The happy smiles on their little faces repaid me many times for the long hours spent working for them.

Different times superintendents would ask me what they could do for me. They didn't want to be always on the receiving end. I would tell them that all I wanted was their prayers. Nearly every letter from all of these foreign groups, or from the children, told me they were praying for me. I am sure that has been a big factor in the success of this work.

When people who work hard every day will get up at 4:30 in the morning to attend prayer meetings and tell me they prayed for me, something has to happen. I could never, never have kept up under the strenuous pace I have maintained for sixteen years without this prayer support. Thanks to my heavenly Father and praying friends.

Often a letter like this from one of "my" pastors would arrive at just the right time to help sustain me. "I pray for you four times every day. I pray that God will bless you and you will live long. My church is going well because of your help to me. But for your help my church might have been closed up. My small church is crowded with members. We have many Sunday School children. Daybreak prayer meetings are full of prayers of confession. One of these five new believers was an idol worshiper. But after conversion the idol was broken up."

Soo Kum always called me her "dear Sis." Others called me their "Mother." One of the fellows was a stamp collector, so we helped each other build up a collection of the other's country's stamps. He sent me many souvenir sheets and late stamps.

I sent one of the girls a handwoven bookmark I had made and she was so thrilled she took it to church to show to people. From the reports, my picture was passed around at church a good many times. A social worker wrote me, "Whenever I see the poor orphan children in the various orphanages, I can hardly keep back the tears. Although you never saw their faces even once, and though the miles separate us, you have helped them spiritually as well as materially like your own children. The superintendent told me that you had sent for these poor ones lots of clothes which you made by yourself. All of them are good articles and cute.

"I was deeply impressed by every line of your letters. Your letter is very kind, encouraging and instructive. It seems to me that you are just like their own mothers. The thing which orphans are longing for mostly is the parent's love.

"Several girls said to me that you are their mother, showing me your picture. I saw that many times the superintendent told orphans that they should work hard in order to repay your Christian neighborliness."

One young Korean interpreter asked me to be his mother as his had been murdered by communists when he was four years old. He wrote, "I am so happy to call you 'mother.' I will be your good son by writing faithfully and by telling you about my work in Compassion. (He had just been offered a job in the office.) I will keep your letter for a long time and will read it over and over. And I will pray for you, especially for your good health.

"I have made up my mind to study well and hard with enthusiasm. I would like to become a good servant, a good ambassador for His gospel. Mother, I hope you will enjoy longevity so that I will invite you to my home when I get married to a nice girl in the future. You will receive our warm greetings of love and I will cook for you, although I am a boy."

I have received seven beautiful Korean lady's dresses and one man's outfit for my father as appreciation gifts from superintendents and social workers. Pink is the color of the girl's engagement ceremony dress and three of the seven I received were pink! My father was a small man and I think the man's suit would have fit Goliath. All the garments were beautifully made by hand and the materials were handsome.

While this work began in Greece and Korea, it has by no means stayed there. It now includes Taiwan, India and Haiti. I sponsored a little boy several years in India under the American Mission to Greeks. His parents were Christians but so poor they could not support him. They wanted him to grow up to be a Christian and become an evangelist. The father was a coolie and made only 18¢ a day—when he could get work. Later, conditions improved for the family and my sponsorship was canceled. In his place I am supporting the Director of Newspaper Evangelism in Sri Lanka who is doing a great work there under the American Mission to Greeks.

There are so many Greek children who needed help, so I asked the AMG for a little girl. Vasiliki Korbakis was assigned to me. She was my little girl for several years. Her parents were both too ill to work to support her so my help was gratefully received. Later they were able to work, so I transferred my support to the Director of Newspaper Evangelism in India.

The poverty is so great in Haiti that I felt I should help a child there. Feda Marseille lives with her parents who are not able to support her. She is so glad for help. Compassion put me in contact there with a missionary under Unevangelized Fields Mission and I have sent her several boxes of clothing for the House of Hope.

Chen Wen Kung, a boy in the Christian Mountain Children's Home at Liu Kwei in Taiwan, was a Chinese boy whom I helped for some time. This

Home is for the very poor aborigine children from the mountains, said to be the poorest people in Taiwan. He was so happy to have a sponsor. I was told that he would hurry home from school in the afternoon and go and look at my picture hanging on the wall.

One Christmas I wrote to the four orphanages I was sending clothing to at the time to send me the number, ages and sex of children who had no sponsors. I gift-wrapped a small gift for each one. There was nothing expensive, just some school and health supplies, small games, articles of clothing, and such things. I never had such fun as I had looking for items I felt they would like and wrapping them in bright colored paper. I generally included a game a number of children could play with together. I received pictures of the children with the gifts, and I tell you, there were some very happy faces. A very happy person looked at the pictures, too. This kind of thrill leaves no bad hangovers.

My latest foreign contact for sewing is India. I am making clothing for the children of national evangelists and Christian workers who are working under "Bibles For The World," whose director is Rochunga Pudaite. Inflation has hit these people in northeastern India very hard and clothing is gratefully received. This is sent to the Wheaton, Illinois office and they send it to India. I have also sent some shipments to India through the AMG. There is no end to the desperate needs everywhere.

It has been such a great joy to be in contact with people of different races and cultures. Some of my dearest friends have strange names and customs, but we are very much alike after all. We also have many problems in common.

This work keeps changing and expanding so that I have no idea what may develop in the future. I had no idea when I retired and began sewing and giving toward the support of orphans and pastors what interesting things would happen to me. I am sure the key to it all was turning my life over to God and permitting Him to direct. He not only showed me how to use my little bucket to do my bit for Him in the world, but, in turn, He showered some of His wonderful blessings on me.

CHAPTER 4

Overflowing in the Orient

Many nights I would lie awake thinking of the various people I had been in contact with in Greece and Korea and sometimes wondering what it would be like to actually visit them in their countries. I never thought it would be possible, of course. I didn't have the nerve to think of trying such a trip.

In the spring of 1966, however—five years after my retirement began—Compassion announced its second Orient tour for sponsors to visit their orphans and see the work being done in the orphanages. What an opportunity that would be for me to visit my orphans! But my father's health was very poor, it looked like his days were numbered, and I couldn't leave him in his condition.

In June, my father went to His eternal home, and a week later I started the proceedings to join the tour. I was going to see Korea!

There was just one "fly in the ointment," and he was a big one. That was the realization that I would have to *fly*. I had never been in a plane and the very thought of it sent shivers down my spine. I always said that no one would ever get me up in one of those things, and I really meant it. I couldn't think of anything urgent enough to tempt me to try it.

Almost before I could realize it myself, I had made my reservation. I was going to see Korea! I was going to one of the far corners of the world to meet people of a strange race whom I had never seen. I would be introduced to foreign cultures, feel the frustration of language barriers, and see face to face for the first time the many people whom I had learned to love from our correspondence.

I'll never forget that winter. We got no instructions for the trip until early in the spring. As I had never gone on a big trip like this would be, I didn't know what to expect—what we would need to take. My imagination worked overtime.

"Will I need this?"

"Should I take that?"

"Is this too warm to wear over there?"

And so it went all winter. All I was sure of was that I must apply for a passport and get the required shots. The realization of what the shots were for anesthetized the sharp pricks. I was going to Korea!

As the time drew nearer to go, my nerves went on such a rampage they affected my health. Medicine didn't help so the doctor put me in the hospital for several days for tests and X rays to see if I was strong enough for the trip.

Nothing serious came to light, so I asked the doctor if my tense nerves were causing the trouble. He smiled and said, "I'm quite sure that is it. When you get started you will be all right."

How right he was.

I prayed many times that winter for God to take away my fear-of-flying complex. I even told Him that if it wasn't His will for me to go, He should make it very clear. Often I would have felt relieved if He had said "No."

As nothing developed to give me reason to think it was not His will, I continued to make the necessary preparations. I packed and unpacked my bags so many times, trying to keep the weight within the 44 pounds limit, it is a wonder everything wasn't worn out. I became quite adept at balancing two traveling bags, a tape recorder, and flight and camera bags on my kitchen scales, all at one time. (When I weighed in at the airport, all they weighed were the two bags. I had been informed that only a handbag was exempt. All that work for nothing!)

Finally, the last day preceding departure was checked off my calendar. The zero hour was at hand. I was standing on the threshold of a never-to-be-forgotten experience. I knew anticipation was running high on both sides of the Pacific.

They say one does not get dying grace until one is ready to die. I found I did not get flying grace until I was ready to fly. When I walked up the ramp of the plane at Tri City airport near my home in Michigan, I was as calm as when I climb on board my little Honda sedan. I was so excited I forgot to take a bromine pill for air sickness before I started. It was a smooth flight and I was never airsick on the whole trip nor on any flights I have taken since. Now I wouldn't want to take a long trip in any other way since I overcame the silly fear of flying.

We met sponsors from the eastern United States and Canada in Chicago and then flew on a Northwest Orient jet to Portland, Oregon, to meet the rest of the group. We numbered 93 people, nearly all of whom were orphan sponsors.

In Portland, we were assigned our roommates. Mine was a pleasant widow from Fresno, California, Mrs. Alice Burnett. We have been close friends ever since. The directors briefed us on things we should know concerning the trip and then we boarded another Northwest jet for a nonstop flight to Japan, where we were to sightsee the first week. I was so excited I almost exploded.

We left Portland in mid-afternoon. I supposed we would be flying at night over that big, deep Pacific

Ocean and I wouldn't have to see all of that water. Instead, we followed the sun all the way and skipped one night. We were high above the clouds all the way and I didn't see the water after all, which helped.

Japan! Our week in Japan was most enjoyable. People were very friendly and gave excellent service. It was difficult to realize that only a few years ago we were such bitter enemies. We had three guides, one lady and two gentlemen, and every day was filled with interest and excitement.

We visited the Mikimoto Pearl Islands where we saw the women pearl divers and a number of women sorting large dishes of pearls. The Noritake china factory was so interesting. The demonstrations at the Toshiba Science Institute were almost unbelievable. We made a trip up into the Japanese Alps where we spent a night at a typical Japanese hotel and rented kimonos to wear in the evening. We saw the Great Buddha of Kamakura and other shrines.

One interesting feature of the tour was the celebration of the birthdays of members of the tour that happened to fall on some day of the trip. As our tour director kept our passports, he knew the dates and had preparations made in advance for the celebrations. Mine fell on a day when we were at the Nagoya International Hotel. My roommate and I were not eating with the others that evening but I was called down to the dining room and they brought in a small birthday cake for me. To cut the cake they provided a huge samurai sword, with a large bow of ribbon tied to the handle. Of course, there was the birthday song, and a gift of fans from the hotel.

A most embarrassing experience happened a short time after we landed in Tokyo. I never wished so hard to be far away from where I was. We had eaten so much on the plane that we were not hungry, but as it was warm four of us ladies thought we would like something cold to eat or drink, not a full meal. We inquired where we could find a place to eat and were directed to the third floor of our hotel.

We went up there and after we were inside we saw it was not a snack bar as we expected. Immediately, several ultra-polite waiters, each with a towel at just the right angle over his arm, bowed us in. None of us knew a polite way to leave.

They led us to a table covered with a spotless white tablecloth. As I was the last to be seated, two waiters almost ran to pull out my chair. Another waiter handed each of us a huge menu card. By the look on his face he was expecting a good order. We told him we wanted only a light lunch. The way he immediately began to remove some of the table service didn't make us feel any happier. I ordered some melon sherbert and a glass of pineapple juice.

We were enjoying ourselves when, what did awkward Eveline do? She knocked over her glass of juice on that spotless tablecloth! Our orders were so small they didn't amount to much and now the whole table had to be changed! Oh, the mental agony of having to call the waiter over. When he saw my empty glass, he asked if I wanted more. I thought, "Horrors, I've had too much already!"

I tried to explain and apologize for the accident. I don't know whether he understood or not. His face never changed expression. We were told not to give any tips on the trip as the cost of the tour included tipping. However, nothing was said about what to do when you spill a glass of juice on a ritzy tablecloth. I felt I must do something, so I left a 50 yen piece at my plate when we left.

We had just had travelers checks changed into Japanese money and I didn't know the value in our money. It must have been adequate, for he made a big bow and smiled from ear to ear. I guess I was forgiven, but I'll never forget my initiation into Japan.

After many exciting adventures the time came to leave the land of the Rising Sun. Another Northwest jet carrying 93 excited people headed into the west across the Sea of Japan to the Land of the Morning Calm, Korea, where many precious children anxiously awaited our arrival.

Coming into Korea two and a half hours later, our plane swept low over the countryside giving us a closeup view of the rice paddies, oriental architecture, and the people. An overwhelming feeling swept over me. I was indeed in a different world.

CHAPTER 5

Face to Face in Korea

We landed at Seoul's Kimpo International Airport and found the building filled with orphans and others who had come to see us. What excitement must have filled those children's hearts as they watched that large jet come in for a landing with their American Mommies and Daddies, the only ones they now had, people who loved them enough to cross the great Pacific Ocean to see them! My two girls were so excited about seeing me. My heart thrills all over again, just thinking about it and all that followed.

An aisle was roped off through the crowd of people so we could get through. As I was halfway through the building, Choo Ill Hwa, a young pen pal social worker, reached over and pinned a corsage on me for the Korea Sung Jo Women's Society in Seoul. When I reached the end of the line, there was my Korean "sis," Joo Soo Kum, a translator—with another corsage! Superintendent Kim Yung Suk and Ill Hwa's boy friend, Mr. Halm, were also there. I was actually seeing, face to face, the ones who had become a part of my life. What joy!

All of us were greeted in true Korean fashion. Huge wreaths of flowers were hung around the necks of Compassion officials who had accompanied us: President Harvey, Dr. Hemwall and their wives, and Mrs. Miriam Swanson, widow of the founder. Two

long rows of little orphans dressed in native
costumes patiently waited for us in the hot sun. Their
faces covered with perspiration, each held a little
corsage in damp hands to give to some member of the
tour. There were three for me. I felt like a walking
florist shop. There was a short program of
welcoming speeches and songs which I recorded to
take home with me.

We were taken to stay at Walker Hill, a resort
complex about one and a half miles from Seoul
which had been built by the U.S. government for our
soldiers stationed in Korea. It consisted of thirty-
seven buildings and five hotels. We were lodged
there because no hotel in Seoul was large enough to
care for all of us on the tour.

The first evening we were served a typical Korean
meal. I never before saw so many vegetables
prepared in so many ways at one meal. There was
rice, of course, and a throat-searing concoction
called *kimchee* which is fermented vegetables with
hot peppers. I just couldn't get it down. This is the
only way some of the people can have raw vegetables
during the winter, but it must be hard on their
stomachs.

Everything was supposed to be eaten with
chopsticks, which didn't help. I was having a
desperate time trying to get enough to eat. It looked
so easy when the Koreans were eating with them, but
I just could not get the knack. I looked around at the
speaker's table and about a half dozen people were
smilingly watching some of our frantic efforts.

When the meal was about half over a waiter
passed forks to those who wanted them. I never
thought a fork could look so good. I don't think I
could ever be a good Oriental when it comes to
eating.

While in Seoul we attended a Mother's Day service

at the Bible Baptist Church. There were 952 children in the Sunday School that morning. The church was trying to reach the more than 35,000 children in the vicinity. An American missionary who had charge of the church preached and a Korean interpreted the sermon for the Koreans. I suspected the interpreter was doing a lot of ad libbing, for it took longer for him to tell it in his language.

Compassion had been renting the building but had just finished their new building which was to be dedicated the last day we were there. Their system of rental was quite unique and interesting. They have to deposit a large sum of money with those from whom they are renting. This money is put out on interest and the interest pays the rent. When one is through renting, the principal amount is returned. Compassion had deposited the sum of $20,000 for this purpose.

En Jeh Hun, one of my translators who knew I would be at the church, came to see me, but the only time we had to talk was while walking several blocks to our bus. He seemed like a fine young man. It was so interesting to know that the translators—those people who served as go-between for the orphan and sponsor—were so interested in meeting the sponsors. This work must mean more to them than just a service.

We visited four main cities: Seoul, Taegu, Pusan and Kwangju. Orphans whose sponsors were on the tour were brought to the city nearest their orphanage to see the sponsors. It happened that the three children I went to see, my two girls and a boy our missionary society was sponsoring, were in the Seoul area, so I met all of them at once. I'll never forget that momentous moment when I saw them coming toward me!

Dear Yung Sook laid her head on my shoulder and

cried like a baby. It was an emotion-filled time for all of us. Counting the three orphans, their interpreters, superintendents, and several others, it made quite a delegation. I received two more large bouquets as well as several gifts. I can't express in words what my feelings were.

Another sponsor had a child at the same orphanage as my Yung Sook, so she was with us. Her little girl was wearing a dress I had made!

It was an emotion-filled time for all of us when I met Yung Sook and her interpreter.

It was pitiful how Yung Sook hung onto me. She was just determined to carry my purse, and I was so afraid someone would snatch it out of her hand. That would have been tragic with the valuable travel documents and money I had in it. The bag had two handles, so finally I let her take one and I held on to the other. The three children hung onto me as though they would never let me go. I needed three arms that afternoon. I have thought since what a pity that some older folks feel so lonely and out of the stream of life when they could experience such love by giving a little of themselves to others who need them.

While we were in the building where we met our orphans, I had an opportunity to take Yung Sook into a room where there was a piano and she played a piece which I taped. She did very well. The superintendents took us to a park in the afternoon and I made some recordings of the children singing.

We wandered around in the grassless park for a time and then we had lunch together. How those people can eat rice! Suh Won Hwa, our missionary society's boy, sat beside me. He was served a huge plate of rice and I wondered how he could ever eat all of it. In just a few minutes not a grain was left.

Yung Sook wanted to talk to me so badly but she was afraid to try her limited English. She handed me a little note telling me what she wanted to say. One of the young interpreters had never known the love of a mother as both his parents had been killed by Communists because they were Christians. He wanted me to be his mother. I told him I would be glad to write to him as a mother, but I couldn't help him financially. He seemed satisfied and happy for the friendship. What sad and lonely hearts war causes, especially among children and young people.

One young translator, the one who came to see me at the church, wrote one time how he felt downgraded socially because he had been brought up in an orphanage, and apologized for it. My heart ached for him. Those of us who have always had a home and parents can't fully realize what those lonely children go through who must live on charity. It is a joy to correspond with them and let them know that someone does care and feels they are worthwhile. The orphanage personnel do a marvelous job caring for these children. So many orphanages, however, are badly overcrowded and it is impossible for them to give each child the love and attention they naturally crave so much.

Late that afternoon Ill Hwa, my young social worker pen pal, her boy friend, Mr. Halm, and an elderly gentleman who had been an interpreter at the American embassy for fifteen years came to Walker Hill after me. For what occasion, I had no idea. We went back to Seoul and stopped in front of a large building. We climbed to the third floor and entered a large room where the Korea Sun Jo Women's Society had assembled to honor me for my work for the orphanages of Korea. What a surprise that was!

Someone gave a speech in English for my benefit and it was translated into Korean. They presented me with an appreciation certificate and a gold medal on a neck chain with the words, "Great Mother," engraved on it. I felt just overwhelmed at their warmhearted recognition for something no more spectacular than making clothing for children. Later a letter of appreciation was sent to me by mail from the Head Man of the province where Superintendent Kim's orphanage is located.

After the recognition ceremony, I was taken to the home of the president of the society for tea. She was not at the meeting but was waiting at home to receive me. We were all seated on cushions on the floor. I was given the honor seat, which had arms. We were served tea in small cups. I don't know what kind of tea it was but it was so hot I could drink only a small amount.

Our hostess was an antique collector. Many of the antiques in her home, I was told, were 500 to 600 years old. I took some pictures of them and she acted as though she felt honored that I would want to.

After all this, I supposed we would be going back to Walker Hill. But not so. There was more to come.

It was time for the evening meal, so the three people who had brought me took me to a restaurant for dinner on the side of a mountain at the edge of the city. There were no sides to the building so we had the full benefit of the cool breeze. I fully enjoyed it after a long day in the heat and dust. We had a good meal and then my new friends returned me to Walker Hill. To say I was tired was the understatement of the year, but it was worth every tired ache.

The day we went to the DMZ—the demilitarized neutral zone between North and South Korea—we had a chance to see something of the hard life of the poorer classes of people. We passed many farmers on their way to town with their loaded pushcarts to sell their farm produce. Often the men were pulling and the wife and children pushing. One could tell from their postures that they were using every ounce of their strength. They seemed to haul everything imaginable that way. Sometimes they would pile furniture and other merchandise on a rack on the back of a bicycle. I don't think I saw half a dozen commercial trucks in that area all the time I was there.

We saw women doing the family wash in recessed pools of water in partially dry river beds. Men were working on roads with shovels and pickaxes. Scaffolding was made of bamboo poles tied together. In spite of these difficulties, there was a great deal of construction going on. We could see it wherever we went. As the country has made much progress in the years since then, I hope they have been able to acquire some of the present day's labor-saving equipment.

That evening, another translator friend, Minja Ahn, came to see me and brought me a little gift. She was planning to be married on Saturday and invited me to the wedding. If I could have attended, I would have had a choice of Korean dresses to wear, for I was soon to receive two. Since it was the last afternoon with my orphans, I couldn't miss being with them, not even for a Korean wedding.

We were now ready to go down country to the three other cities to greet the orphans at Taegu, Pusan and

One translator, Soo Kum, sent me a picture of her engagement ceremony.

54

Kwangju. Since no hotels in the cities were large enough to accommodate all of us, and the one plane at our disposal couldn't handle that many, we were divided into two groups. We were all to go to the same places but on different days. They informed us that we were allowed to take only our flight bags for the three days. And anything else we could carry. I interpreted that freely and carried, in addition to my flight bag, my large handbag, camera supply bag and a tape recorder. Our large bags were collected for

The stamp collector translator, Lee Chul Woo, wanted me to see his sweet bride.

55

storing until we came back and it made quite a mountain of luggage since most of the 93 people in the tour had brought the allotted two bags each.

Our group arrived at Taegu at about 10 o'clock in the morning. Many orphans and superintendents, with other personnel and interpreters, were there to meet us. Several of "my family" were waiting to greet me. "Timothy" Kim Ki Poong, one of the pastors I was supporting, and his interpreter, as well as Kim Eun Yung and his family were there. Timothy's interpreter was a columnist for the English Daily in Seoul and Kim Eun Yung was translator for Mrs. Bae's orphanage. As there were no patrons at the Tourist Center at that hour in the morning, we were allowed to visit together there.

Timothy's wife had made me a beautiful Korean dress with accessories and sent them with her husband. (He had asked for my measurements before I went on the trip.) I slipped the dress on over my suit and we took a lot of pictures. They all seemed to want to have a picture taken with me. I made some tapes of the twin sons of Eun Yung singing, and some of the conversations going on. I wanted so badly to talk directly with Soon Ae, Eun Yung's wife. She was such a sweet person.

This little family gave me several nice gifts: three interesting good luck charms, a tin box of candy, and a brass lacquered vase with a wooden pedestal decorated with mother-of-pearl. I looked at the pedestal, with its four seven-inch legs, and wondered how I could get it in my bulging luggage.

People who have never traveled on a large scale do not realize how limited a traveler's luggage is. I already was carrying the four bags, now how was I to manage a large unwieldy box containing the dress, slip and rubber dress shoes, the smaller gifts tied up in a babushka, and the vase and four-legged pedestal?

But the gifts were given out of their hearts of love. They wanted to do something for me to show their appreciation for the things I had tried to do for them. I was grateful for every token of their love and I would manage—someway. Fortunately, a special bus took us to the different places we were to see and we could leave our luggage on the bus. Alice and others on the tour helped me manage all my possessions on the bus—and later on the train to Pusan.

I still correspond with Eun Yung's little family. They write to me as if I were their mother. Of course, Eun Yung does the writing as only he speaks English, but I am sure his sweet wife and his sons tell him some things to say.

We visited orphanages in the Taegu area and the Presbyterian hospital there, and then left for Pusan. It was late in the afternoon and the mountains were throwing long shadows across the countryside. Our diesel train was all that broke the stillness—not an automobile was in sight. Here and there we could see a little hut some farmer called home. We passed many rice paddies and could see farmers at work in them, and sometimes someone was leading home a cow or two. There were many fruit trees in this section. It was the most peaceful scene I had witnessed in years.

More than two and a half hours later we reached Pusan. It was dark. Eun Yung who had traveled with us in order to interpret for another orphan in Pusan, rounded up Rev. and Mrs. Bae from the crowd at the station. Mrs. Bae, you may recall, took her husband's place as superintendent of an orphanage where I sent clothing for a number of years when her husband took on other responsibilities.

The Baes were so friendly and gave me such

hearty handclasps. Mrs. Bae had a large bundle under her arm, which she let me know through Eun Yung was a dress for me. But she didn't give it to me and I wondered why. And then the thought struck me—another dress to *pack!*

After the greetings were over, we were taken to the Tognae Tourist Hotel at the edge of Pusan where I was grateful to be able to deposit my collection of luggage. This hotel had four floors and no elevators. That is, they had first, second, third and fifth floors, but no fourth. It would have been considered bad luck to have a fourth floor. I learned that it was the same way in hospitals.

After we sponsors had breakfast, the orphans, interpreters and superintendents began to arrive. Soon the Baes and Eun Yung made their appearance with smiles. Then Mrs. Bae presented me with her gift. That's right, it was another beautiful Korean dress—a pink one! And, of course, there was a slip and rubber shoes to go with the dress.

Mrs. Bae and I went into one of the rooms and I slipped the pink dress on over my suit (Korean dresses are very full), and she and I had our pictures taken. (After I came home I had a picture enlarged for her and she wrote me she was so proud of it she put it on her desk so everyone could see it.)

We went on a little sightseeing trip down to the harbor and then back to the hotel for lunch. The sponsors were to be the hosts and hostesses for this meal for their guests. I told my guests they could order either an American or a Korean meal. They all chose American. Everyone did very well except Mrs. Bae. She just couldn't get her hamburger down. I thought, "You dear soul. I couldn't get your kimchee down, either."

In the afternoon, with a police escort for our buses, we made a social call on the mayor. We went dashing down the main street of Pusan with sirens blowing and "Compassion Orient Tour" banners billowing in the wind. Everyone in our path quickly moved over—we had the right of way. If any vehicle came near, the escort motioned it over with his thumb, and everyone obeyed. But it was funny to see people looking to see who the "dignitaries" were! We were visiting the mayor of Pusan, of course!

We were seated in the council room. After everyone was properly welcomed and thanked for the help they had given, which was deeply appreciated, we were served tea. Then each of us was presented a Pusan pin.

Then we visited an orphanage where Dr. and Mrs. Hemwall were sponsoring two boys. A birthday party had been planned for the boys, and all of us were guests at the party. We had to leave our shoes outside the door and sit at low tables about a foot high. We sat on cushions and put our feet under the table. After a few minutes, I was in sheer agony. If I leaned to one side, the arthritis in my right knee complained. If I turned the other way, I had a kink in my side.

Two birthday cakes with candles were served, also candy, cookies and apples. Dr. Hemwall was a medical doctor and had brought along a supply of medicine in case any of us became ill—which was a comforting thought! Since Dr. Hemwall was sponsoring this party, I felt it would be safe to eat some of the treat.

Eating is a problem for foreign travelers over there. All water that is taken internally must be boiled before we can use it. We couldn't brush our teeth without boiled water, which was furnished by our hotels. All fruit and vegetables had to be either cooked or peeled. Dr. Hemwall gave us a rule that if it couldn't be cooked or peeled, don't eat it. They do not use chemical fertilizer and the kind they do use makes food unsafe for those not used to it.

The little girls on my side of the table at the party began sugaring everyone's coffee. One little girl would lick off her fork and stick it in the sugar bowl and lick it off. That tasted so good she had to have another lick. I was glad I wasn't eating anything that required sugar!

I decided I must take some pictures, which gave me a chance to get up and relieve my cramped muscles. It seemed, though, that a "good time was had by all," in spite of some of us not being accustomed to sitting on the floor.

That evening I had to make an effort to consolidate my luggage. Everything had to be emptied and repacked. My handbag was already full, which is its normal condition, but the camera supply bag was beginning to have a bit of extra space. It took some doing, but I crammed two dresses and shoe outfits into a box meant for one outfit. Korean dresses are very full and the lining makes them heavier.

It was the pedestal with its four legs that was the headache to pack. I never tried to pack anything so non-cooperative. Those seven-inch legs stuck out like the drumsticks of a trussed Thanksgiving turkey. They could not be pressed down or shaken together. After much effort I managed to rearrange the things filling my flight bag and at last everything was under cover. Those poor bags looked as if they were suffering from advanced cases of the gout. I decided that if I ever took another trip I would pack a collapsible shopping bag when I left home.

Kwangju was our last stop and this was the only city we visited where no one was there to meet me. I really felt lost. We visited more orphanages and listened to their programs which were always delightful—I never tired of listening to them. Many chuckles from the audience mingled with the voices of the little singers.

They do not need a line or two of their songs to get them warmed up. They explode on the first word. Oriental children love to sing, and these did not seem a bit bashful and sang like it was very important business.

Programs had been prepared for us in almost all of the orphanages we visited. Some of the music was instrumental. One young fellow played a number on the piano that he planned to play in a competition. I am sure he must have been a winner.

The children all seemed to know two English words, and how they shouted "Hello" and "Goodbye" to us as we arrived and left! I was so sorry I didn't have a chance to see the orphanages I had made clothing for. They were too far from where we were and the schedule was very tight. I met all of the superintendents and one brought a child to represent the rest. How I did want to see all of them.

Back in Seoul, the moments of our stay in Korea were fast coming to an end. After supper twelve bus loads of sponsors and Koreans made their way to the airport for our last goodbyes. Yung Sook was the only one of my orphans to get back to see me again. We rode together and her little hand was in mine all the way to the airport. The nearer we came, the sadder her face became. We climbed to the second floor of the airport where many "Thank you's" and firm handclasps were shared over and over.

Finally, the time came for us to part. We formed two large circles and, with clasped hands, we sang— or tried to sing—"God be with you till we meet again," knowing that for most of us, there would be no "again" in this world.

Then the zero hour came and we made our way out

It was sad to part with Yung Sook (right) and Won Hwa, the boy supported by our missionary society. Soon Ja (left) was wearing an outfit I made.

into the night to board our waiting plane. Our Korean friends waved and watched us as far as they could see. It was an emotion-filled time for all of us. The curtain had come down on the most tremendous week of my life, a week that will live in my memory as long as life lasts. I felt just limp after it was over.

But I had one more task to care for before I could settle down for the flight. Superintendent Kim had given me two shopping bags of souvenirs his orphans had made for the sponsors and he asked me to give them out after we were aboard the plane. Several of the other sponsors kindly helped me handle all my luggage by each taking a piece of it. I suppose I am remembered as the lady who always had so much luggage she didn't know what to do.

CHAPTER 6

The Long
Way Home

We had to return to Tokyo to get our plane for home. But we would not be flying straight back to the States. We were to have a visit in Hong Kong. As I settled back for the flight to Tokyo, I thought how happy all of us on the tour must feel to have had this wonderful opportunity to visit those we had helped to support in money and gifts and prayer.

I wondered if perhaps I had even more to rejoice over than most of the other tour members. Nearly all of them had made the trip to see one person, and after that contact had been made, the highlight of their trip had been experienced. For me, I had been on the mountaintop all the time I was in Korea. As I thought it over I counted thirty-eight people who had made a special effort to see me and each meeting with them was exciting for both them and me. I had missed seeing only two of "my people"— Lee Yo Sup and Lee Chul Woo.

The next morning we left on a Cathy Pacific plane for Hong Kong. It was Sunday and we had a church service on the plane. Dr. Hemwall, who conducted our regular morning devotions, gave an inspirational message, a lady sang a solo, and some girls gave testimonies. It was so nice to have this time of worship as we flew through the clouds.

Hong Kong was another exciting experience. We

were taken on a trip around Hong Kong Island, and in a hydrofoil boat to the floating Aberdeen Sea Palace Restaurant, where we were served an eight-course Chinese dinner. The harbor was filled with sampans, junks, and large ships from many nations. We visited Tiger Balm Gardens, the Disneyland of the East. We saw the Walled City, and were in the New Territories on the mainland China up to the bamboo curtain. I'll never forget the fishmarket "cologne"!

We were in Hong Kong two nights and parts of three days. It was 1967, the days of the bad rioting, so we were not allowed out of the hotel after dark. Since we had some time for shopping, I decided to mail a box of clothing and gifts home so I would have room in my bags for things I would buy. Every time Alice and I would come back to our room after finding some more things we couldn't live without, the place looked like a tornado had struck it. We would empty our bags and repack them to try to crowd in something else.

Our next stop was the Philippines, where we would take a plane for the Hawaiian Islands. While waiting for the plane we were given a tour of the City of Manila.

When we reached Hawaii, we were officially "home," and had to go through Customs and show our passports. I dreaded this, for rumors had been going around about how luggage is messed up when inspection is made. After all it had taken to get my things packed into the bags, I had visions of trying to do it all over again at the Customs table.

On other previous landings, our tour guide presented our passports, but here we were required to show them ourselves. It turned out, however, that they gave all of us just a token inspection. Being a missionary group, they seemed to give us credit for not trying to smuggle in contraband. The inspector opened my bags just enough to take a peek inside and waved me on.

When we went outside we were given the full Hawaiian greeting—a beautiful lei, and kisses of greeting from a swarthy Hawaiian man for the ladies and from a Polynesian girl for the men.

Alice and I had a wonderful room with cross ventilation. A strong breeze was blowing, which was a heavenly change after the heat and humidity of Hong Kong. The hotels had such romantic names: "The Trade Wind," "The Breakers," "The Reef," and ours, "The Coral Seas." While here we were given both tours and free time.

We took a tour of the Island, including Pearl Harbor; stopped at a pineapple plantation for a treat of juicy ripe pineapples; visited the Polynesian Culture Center; and went through a rain forest.

On our free day we went shopping, and oh, how I could have used a U-Haul trailer! We went to Hawaii's largest shopping mall, at that time considered the largest in the world. The many things made from monkey pod wood were beautiful. Did I ever have some re-packing to do after that trip! We also went to the International Market and down to Waikiki Beach.

Then came the last day, and what a tiresome day it was! All planned events were over, and we were just marking time until 10:30 that evening when the tour was to be officially completed. It turned out to be a distressing afternoon. We had to give up our rooms at 12:00 o'clock noon, so the hotel gave us a few courtesy rooms in which to rest and clean up.

We were all exhausted. The excitement that had kept us going was over and we just wilted. Before the end of the afternoon, the beds were full, and the chairs and floor had sprawling forms all over them.

The lobby of the hotel was a sight with 180-plus bags waiting to be trucked to the airport for the last time. Finally, 9:00 o'clock came and most of us went out to board our buses, also for the last time.

Another smooth flight brought us to Seattle. There we had the first plane trouble of the entire trip. The landing gear wouldn't come down mechanically so we had to circle the city while the copilot worked it down manually. He finally made it work and we landed without incident. But a fire truck was waiting there—just in case! Due to this we had to change planes and those with a tight flight schedule missed connections. I had extra time so it didn't affect me. Not many went with me to Chicago and Tri City.

The Midland airport taxi was at the Tri City airport waiting, so I was soon at home. I don't think Midland ever looked so good. I was nearly dead from exhaustion and it took several months to recuperate from the strain, but it was worth it. How good God was to take such wonderful care of us on this trip.

Not long after the trip I had to discontinue sending clothing to Korea as the government began charging heavy duty to discourage people from sending such things into the country. They wanted their people to buy their own manufactured clothing and thus stimulate their own economy. I could understand that, but I was sorry, as the orphanages still needed help. I have lost contact with a number of the people for various reasons, but others have taken their places.

I considered this my "once in a lifetime" trip. I felt it was a wonderful blessing from God, sent me for helping poor helpless orphans. I would never have made the trip if I hadn't had the contact in Korea as a result of my "retirement" work. How little I realized that this was just the beginning of greater things to come.

CHAPTER 7

Overflowing in Europe

Another trip anywhere was certainly not on my agenda for a good long time. After returning home I was content to be quiet and recuperate from the Orient Tour and just glory in that tremendous experience. I needed time to let my purse recuperate, too. But almost before I knew it I was deep into plans to visit Europe the coming summer.

For several years my Greek friend, Elpitha Markoglou, had been urging me to come to Greece and visit her. She was working with Mr. and Mrs. Mark Diavastes, the couple in charge of the orphanage in Katerini, Greece, where I sent my first box of clothing five years before I retired. Macedonia Bible Institute was a part of Katerini Orphanage and a young woman by the name of Elpitha Markoglou was teaching English at the Institute.

I had read about Elpitha's work in the American Mission to Greeks literature I received. It seemed she was not getting enough financial support. I felt a strong urge to write to her as I thought I might be able to help her in some way.

I sent to AMG headquarters for her address, something I had never done before and have never done since. She and her mother both wrote such nice letters to me and we have been like sisters ever since. My, that all began twelve years ago!

Elpitha became the Director of Child Evangelism

in Greece and twice visited the United States for deputation work. I had the joy of entertaining her in my home both times. After she learned I had been to Korea, she really put pressure on me to make the trip to Greece. I had always been scared to death at the thought of making such a big trip alone, in a foreign country where I did not know one word of their language. Yes, I had gone to Korea, but that was with a tour and under the protection of the tour leaders.

Then Elpitha wrote that there was going to be a Biennial European Child Evangelism conference for all the free countries of Europe, South Africa, Australia and the United States to be held in the Netherlands. She urged me to meet her there and travel down to Greece with her and her mother when the conference was over.

I told her I didn't feel it would be possible but I would pray about it. I figured that if it was God's will, He would open the way. I must confess I didn't pray very hard, for my get-up-and-go had about all got up and went.

But Elpitha would not give up. She wrote that the Diavastes, who had moved back to the States some years before, were going to give their daughter, Ruth, a trip back to Greece as a high school graduation gift. She suggested that I write and see if I could travel with them.

I had never met the family and I didn't have the nerve to write them. I was afraid that my going with them might complicate their plans. But Elpitha wrote them, and it wasn't long before I received a very cordial letter inviting me to travel with them. Mr. Diavastes and Ruth were flying to London and would go down to Brussels, Belgium. He would buy a Volkswagen and they would drive down through eastern Europe, be in Greece for several weeks, and then drive back to London through western

Europe—and I was invited to go with them. When I finished reading that letter, I think I could have been knocked over with a toothpick.

I didn't know what in the world to do. How could I afford another big trip? How would three generations of people, who had never met, get along under perhaps difficult traveling conditions? Would they have to change their plans to accommodate me? My brain was in a whirl.

Through it all a voice seemed to say, "It's now or never." There wasn't a chance in a million that I would ever have such a fantastic opportunity again.

I decided to go. The people at the Teacher's Credit Union just love to loan money, and I knew they would loan me what I lacked for expense. My passport was still valid and I didn't need any shots. I had just a few weeks to prepare. The last few days I went around almost in a daze. But this time I was not afraid of flying.

As the Child Evangelism conference was about the time the Diavastes were leaving, I decided to go on alone and meet Elpitha in the Netherlands, travel to her home in Greece with her and meet Mr. Diavastes and Ruth when they were ready to leave Greece. I was afraid two long trips in a small car would be too much for me.

If I had known just how rugged a trip it was going to be, I never would have gone for I would have thought I couldn't stand it. I am glad I didn't know, for God gave me the strength to stand the furious pace of the trip. I found that His promise is true: "As thy days, so shall thy strength be" (Deuteronomy 33:25). I certainly needed His strength every day and He gave it.

One of the most frightening experiences of my life, and the one that proved that God takes care of little old ladies, was the first day in the Netherlands. I left

Tri City airport on the afternoon of July 12, and arrived in Amsterdam by 6:30 our time the next morning in a light rain. It was 11:30 A.M. Amsterdam time. If I had dreamed the events of the first hours there, I would have called it a nightmare.

I dreaded most the first part of the trip, for I had to take a train for Utrecht, and a bus from there to Woudshoten, the conference center. And I had to do it alone. I couldn't have spoken one word of Dutch if my life had depended on it. I was given directions about how to find the places, but when I am in a strange place about the only direction I am sure of is straight up, which isn't much help.

A bus was waiting at the airport to take passengers to the depot uptown, so I was able to reach the train station without any trouble. I checked my bag and didn't know until later that people seldom check their luggage as they are afraid it will be stolen. I had a travelers check changed into guilders. Then the nightmare began.

I got my ticket and began to look for my train. There were several in the yard but I couldn't find anyone who could tell me which was mine. I couldn't see any train officials anyplace. I went over tracks, climbed stairs, asking and not being understood, until I was almost frantic. Finally, a waiting passenger told me which train was mine.

I lost no time getting on, but then I didn't know which coach I was supposed to be in. I sampled several until I found a nice compartment and settled down in it. Before long several Dutch people came into the compartment. Each of them gave me a puzzled look, but I couldn't understand what I was doing wrong. Their continuing looks made me feel very uneasy.

Soon the conductor came in and looked at my ticket and asked, "Did you ask for a first class ticket?" Then I understood. The Dutch people had reserved that compartment for themselves and couldn't understand why I was there. I explained to the conductor that it was the first time I had ever been in Europe and I didn't know where to go. He permitted me to keep my seat as it wasn't needed by the others. I was grateful, but I felt embarrassed all the way to Utrecht.

When I reached Utrecht, I was told where the buses would stop and I went there. There wasn't a bus in sight and nothing there to indicate it was a bus stop. I inquired of several gatekeepers but I couldn't understand what they told me.

I went to the baggage room to see if my bag had come. No bag. Back again to look for the bus. No bus, either. Back again to the baggage room. Still no bag. I had heard that sometimes baggage doesn't come until a later train. I didn't know what in the world I would do if the bag didn't come until the next day. Now when I hear people talk about being at "Wits' End Corner," I know just what the place looks like.

I think the gate men probably understood and were trying to answer me, but so much Dutch had rubbed off on their English I couldn't recognize it. Finally I asked for someone who could speak English and was directed to the Information desk. A young woman went with me to the baggage room and while we were trying to decide what to do, one of the trainmen walked in with my bag. I never thought a traveling bag could look so heavenly! The young woman told me where to wait for the bus.

I carried my heavy bag over there and then began a long wait. I was informed by the conference guide book that either bus #17 or #54 would take me to my destination. I don't know how long I stood there. Several buses came in but not mine. I tried to learn from bystanders what time my bus was due, but the only answer was a shrug of the shoulders and a shake of the head. I was learning that meant they didn't understand.

Finally a bus came in with the name "Zeist" on it. I remembered that this was the name of a village near the conference and I wondered if by some chance it might take me there. It was worth a try. I had a problem getting the bus driver to understand what I wanted to know. Finally I pointed to the bus and to the name in my conference book and he seemed to understand and nodded his head. I paid my fare and boarded the bus. I was feeling quite pleased with myself that I had been able to get a bus even though it was different from those I was directed to.

The driver told me when to get off. The place didn't look at all the way I thought it would from the description in the book. I asked a lady waiting at the bus stop if we were in Woudshoten and she acted as though she had never heard of the place. I nearly collapsed.

I didn't have the least idea where I was or how to get to where I wanted to go. The only thing I could think of doing was to wait there until one of the buses I should take would come by. It didn't dawn on me until months later that very likely the bus I needed didn't go on that route at all!

It was late in the afternoon and I hadn't eaten a bite since breakfast with the exception of a piece of candy the Dutch people in my compartment had offered me as they passed a box around. I was tired and terribly worried. How I prayed! Several buses stopped, but not mine. I stood there until five o'clock and watched many cars and motorcycles whiz past, probably carrying people home from work.

My attention kept being attracted toward a large white house just across from the bus stop. There were a number of older men around the place and there seemed to be considerable activity going on. I finally worked up enough nerve to lug my bag across the street. Perhaps they would have a telephone so I could call the conference for help.

I knocked on the door and an elderly gentlemen answered. "Does anyone here speak English?" I asked. He shook his head no. Just then a lady came to the door and said, "I do." That was the best "I do" I had ever heard!

As I was explaining my predicament to her, her husband came into the room, evidently just arriving home. She told him about my problem and he said, "I'll take her there."

My relief was too great to express in words. He and his son put my luggage in their car and took me right to the door of the conference building. He wouldn't take a guilder for his trouble. I have since thought that the place must have been a home for pensioners since there were so many older men around. How thankful I was that I had braved going across the street to it.

When we arrived at the conference I understood why I had had such a hectic afternoon. I learned that if I had taken the right bus and had been left off at the right bus stop, I would have had to walk a quarter mile through the woods, carrying my luggage, which I never could have done. There was no place where I could have obtained transportation except for what looked like a tavern across the road. So my wonderful heavenly Father guided me to a bus that would stop right across from what was, perhaps, the only place in the area where people understood English and were in a position to help me.

What had looked like only knots and tangles in the tapestry of life I had been weaving now looked like a wonderful picture of God's guiding care. I consider it one of the high spots of my Christian experience. No matter how small or insignificant we may be, if we are His children, He will not desert us in our time of need. I still thank Him from my whole heart every time I think of the experience.

It so happened that Elpitha and her mother had been in Utrecht about the same time I was there and had arrived at the conference just a few minutes before I did. I had so hoped someone would meet me, but I feel God didn't allow it as He wanted to show me He could take care of me without her help.

Elpitha is my special Greek friend.

I deeply enjoyed the conference, which lasted a week. Seventeen nationalities were represented among more than 100 people attending. The missionaries were all so friendly. The building was huge and part of it was a dormitory, so we lived there. We all ate together. Our place cards were changed daily so we had a chance to get acquainted with many people.

There was a lady from South Africa I dreaded to sit beside—and I was placed beside her twice. I don't know how she got enough to eat as she seemed to be talking all the time. She would turn and face me and rattle on with her thick Dutch accent and I scarcely understood anything she said. Then she would stop and expect me to say something. Maybe she had asked me a question, I don't know. How in the world do you know what to say if you have no idea what has been said? I would smile and nod my head, desperately hoping I was nodding it in the right direction. God only knows what all I nodded assent to.

All the meetings were in English, but a few needed interpreting. The reports were very interesting. It was encouraging to know what was being done in other countries to win boys and girls to Christ.

Our afternoons were free and I had a chance to see some very interesting places. We visited an old castle, Delft, the Zuider Zee, Hilversum—known as the Hollywood of the Netherlands. We saw the Queen's summer palace, and some typical Dutch costumes and country. Again I felt I was in another world.

When the week was over, some missionaries took Elpitha and her mother, an Austrian missionary, and me as far as Frankfort. We went by train to Munich and then to Venice, Italy. About fifteen tiring hours. It was fun taking a canal boat ride on one of the main canals in Venice.

After a day in Venice we had a long thirty-hour continuous train ride through Communist Yugoslavia, Italy and Greece. Riding trains in Europe is a real experience. Going through Yugoslavia, there was a fist fight in our compartment between the conductor and a passenger. Elpitha pushed both of them through the door and out into the corridor and closed the door! I wondered what I would have done had I been traveling alone. Another time we were held up for an hour while the train was searched for a thief.

We finally reached Thessaloniki, Greece. The Apostle Paul wrote two letters to the first century church in this city—the epistles, I and II Thessalonians, in our Bible. This was the home of Elpitha and her mother. We arived about midnight. How good it was to be able to move around again. Elpitha's home was in a large apartment building and each apartment had a small balcony. It was across the street from an outdoor restaurant and it was interesting to watch the people come and go.

Elpitha took me to see many interesting places, but the orphanages were of topmost interest to me. We went to Katerini orphanage, the first one I sent clothing to, but I was disappointed to find that the children were at camp. We visited Melissia orphanage in Thessaloniki, where Elpitha held Bible classes. There were only fifteen girls there, as the rest were at camp.

They knew we were coming and were sitting outside doing the most beautiful embroidery work I have ever seen done by young hands. It was fine cross stitch, done on very fine linen without a pattern stamped on it. The stitches covered two of the fine threads. Some of the pieces were almost covered with designs. Some of their unfinished work was almost unbelievable. They sell their work to help with the expense of the orphanage and I bought a small piece.

We went through the building and found the rooms very clean but so barren of the extra things that make a home out of a house. The bedrooms consisted of twenty narrow or bunk beds, and a stove. The beds had no pillows. In one room the cots were so close the girls had to climb in bed over the foot. That spring I had worked on many comforters earlier than usual, and had fourteen finished. When I saw the barren beds, I knew why. When I returned home I finished six more and sent them to this orphanage so one room could have new ones. It gave me a lot of personal pleasure to know that these girls would have colorful beds as well as warm ones to snuggle into at night.

After a week with Elpitha and her mother we drove to a Christian rest camp by the side of the Aegean Sea near Alexandroupolis, close to the Turkish border. On the way we stopped at the ancient city of Philippi and I walked around the ruins. There were remains of the ancient market stalls and I tried to imagine the Apostle Paul shopping—and preaching—in those market places. I went down in the dungeon where it is thought he was imprisoned. It gave me a very strange feeling.

It was so peaceful here and restful. I often wished I could communicate with the Greek Christians. All women under 65 years of age were expected to help in the kitchen with meals and clean up. I wanted to take my turn but they wouldn't let me. Maybe they were afraid I wouldn't know how to wash dishes in Greek.

I so enjoyed sitting out on the little balcony of our cottage watching the ripple of moonlight on the shimmering waves of the Aegean Sea. Sometimes I felt like pinching myself to see if I was really there in person. Our room faced the sea on two sides so we had a wonderful view. It was fun to walk around on the beach and I did a lot of beach combing. One day I took my shoes off and waded in the sea.

Nearly everyone at the camp went swimming but there was no parading around in swim suits. The women wore a dress over the swim suit down to the beach and put it on again before they came back to camp.

On August 10th Elpitha, her mother and aunt took

me to Alexandroupolis to catch a plane to Athens. There I would join the Diavastes on the long trek back to London. My seatmate was a young man from the island of Crete who knew a little English and told me the names of the islands as we flew over them. At Athens he helped me off the plane with my bags and on to the bus which took us up to the terminal. It was dark as we came into Athens and it is a beautiful city at night with so many colored lights. We could see the Acropolis on top of a mountain lighted with flood lights.

The plane was late getting into Athens and there was no one there to meet me at the terminal. I waited, feeling anxious, for I did not have their address and didn't know where they might be. When he arrived nearly an hour later, Mr. Diavastes said he had been informed the plane would be later than it was.

Mr. Diavastes had secured a room for me with a lovely Christian lady who was an interpreter. He took me to her home in a taxi and she met me with outstretched arms. Our last names gave each other difficulty so we were "Sophia" and "Eveline" as long as I was there.

We were in Athens three days and enough was crowded into that time to last a week. I learned how much I could take without breaking. The next morning being Sunday, Sophia invited me to go to church with her. We had to walk a long distance to take a bus, then another bus and more walking. I thought we would never arrive. When we did, the organist wasn't there so I was asked to play the old pump organ.

The bellows must have been about worn out for I had to pump for dear life to keep the music from dying. Their songs have four to eight stanzas and they always sing all of them—very slowly. There are no slighted third stanzas in Greece. By the time the music part of the service was over I was almost exhausted. Sophia interpreted the sermon for me very quietly so I knew what it was about. It is very tiresome to listen to a long sermon in another language and not have the slightest idea what is being said. I appreciated her thoughtfulness.

The pastor and his wife, who were entertaining the Diavastes, had included me in an invitation for dinner. In the afternoon we went to the museum but it was closed. We window-shopped for a time and then took a bus to the Acropolis.

We climbed steps and inclines until we reached the top of the hill where the Greek temples had been built. As the sun beat down unmercifully, we clambered over ruin after ruin. We climbed marble steps that had been worn smooth from the millions of feet that have walked over them through the centuries and stood on Mars Hill, where Paul preached.

Afternoons are so hot during July and August in Athens that stores close and people go to bed and sleep as they do at night. It is considered a misdemeanor to make undue noise then, and a person can be fined for it. That was the kind of afternoon it was when we were visiting the Acropolis. My face was so hot I was afraid of sunstroke. I found a shady place behind a column and rested awhile, then we all sat in the seats of the remains of the Amphitheater where the old Greek plays were performed.

Mr. Diavastes finally found some popsicles for sale and bought one for each of us. That helped some, but they melted so quickly and got on our hands— and I hated to touch my camera with my sticky hands, so I didn't get as many pictures there as I wanted. After we came down from the Acropolis we found a place to buy iced lemonade. I used a piece of ice from my glass to wash the stickiness from my hands. When we arrived in the center of Athens, we sat down gratefully in an outdoor restaurant and ordered more lemonade. They just brought us the fixings and we had to make our own! No ice.

That evening we were to meet our hosts at another church where there was to be a union service between two churches. It was supposed to be quite a special occasion, but it was an hour of pure torture for me. The organ was out of tune and the organist and congregation had a time trying to keep together on those long songs. I was so dead tired I didn't see how I could sit through the service. If I could have understood the speaker, it would have helped the time to pass more quickly.

At the close of the service there was an announcement that there would be an hour of fellowship in the basement. So for another hour I sat with a group of people I could converse with very little, and then Sophia and I had that long walk and the bus rides back to her apartment.

Sophia was so interested in the work I was doing for orphans that we sat up for nearly another hour talking about it. Then the day mercifully ended. Or so I thought. There had been a wedding in the neighborhood that day and there was still a great deal of celebrating going on with loud singing and crying. They were really pulling out all the stops until someone called the police, who came and put a stop to it.

Yes, I really learned how much this "retired" woman could take without breaking. But I'll never forget my Sunday in Athens.

I didn't feel really rested the next morning but had to get up and get going. After much telephoning Sophia contacted the orphanage where I had been sending clothing for a few years and made an appointment for us to visit it at six that evening. I wanted to take the girls some sweets so we went to a small shop nearby. I didn't realize we were not coming back to the apartment before going to the orphanage so I didn't take my slide camera with me and had only two shots left on black and white film. I was so disappointed, as I wanted pictures of that orphanage more than anything else in Greece.

Thirteen girls lived in this orphanage under the direction of a widow lady. I will remember the greeting I received from this dear matron to my dying day. She almost ran when she saw me and threw her arms around me and hugged me within an inch of my life. All the precious girls filed past me and kissed my hand, the Greek way of greeting. The girls sang several songs for us and the matron peeled fruit for refreshments. She took us through the buildings and they were the homiest I have ever seen. How I wanted my camera. The two pictures I did take in black and white weren't good.

The girls almost stripped their rose garden of blooms for a bouquet for me. They were all wearing the dresses I had sent them in the spring. Each dress fitted as if I had tried them on the girls as I made them. What a wonderful time that was. I felt paid a dozen times for all the time spent sewing for them. I hated to leave. The girls all kissed my hand again in farewell and I got another big hug from the matron.

Early the next morning Sophia and I started out to see if we could find little Vasiliki Korbakis, whom I was sponsoring. I had been invited to go with the Diavastes and friends of theirs to an evangelical camp for children at Sunion, almost at the southernmost tip of Greece later that day, so we had to make this trip early in the morning. Since we were leaving Greece the next day, it was now or not at all. I was very anxious to see this child. She was not an orphan but her parents were not physically able to work and she needed support.

We had obtained her address from the AMG office in Athens but we couldn't locate her. We learned later that her last name had been misspelled and the neighbors didn't recognize it. We were almost ready to give up when a man across the street saw us and came over to ask us if we were looking for someone. Who do you suppose he was? Little Vasiliki's uncle! Of all the people on the street he would be the one to contact us. It was a very unusual thing for him to do. I know it was God who directed him for He wanted the child and me to have the joy of seeing each other. The uncle told us she was in the hospital and had just had an operation for brain tumor. The hospital was within walking distance.

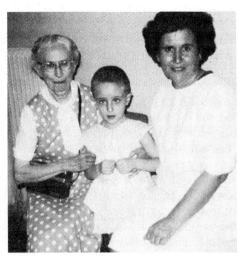

We found little Vasiliki in a hospital.

We found that the child was able to walk and that her mother "happened" to be there. I am sure God planned that, also. Her mother brought her down to the office and we had a short visit and had our picture taken together.

I had brought some clothing for Vasiliki that I made for her and she was so happy with it she clasped it to her breast as if it were a doll. I had planned to buy her a doll but we visited her before the stores were open. I gave Sophia money to buy one for Vasiliki after I left. I had such a nice letter from the mother when I returned home. She said it seemed like a wonderful dream that we had a chance to see each other. Later the father's health improved and he was able to take a job so my sponsorship was discontinued.

The trip to Sunion was very enjoyable. It was a drive of about 75 miles along the blue Aegean Sea and the sky was cloudless. The camp was a very nice one with a large number of children. I discovered that little Greek children can react in very much the same way as American youngsters do. There was a water fountain in one corner of the yard and when the girls came to get a drink, the boys would come over and squirt water on them. It was a very familiar scene to this ex-schoolteacher. When one of the women saw what was going on, she made a scatterment just like our women would do. We are very much the same after all.

On the way back we stopped at a restaurant and were treated to a fish dinner. In Greece the heads and fins are left on the fish when they are cooked. The head is considered the best part of the fish. Even the eyes are left in and eaten. Whenever I was served a whole fish I always gave the head away and I never had any trouble in disposing of it. It took my appetite away to see those dull eyes staring up at me. I was thankful to see that Ruth and her father didn't eat them either, so I had company.

When our host was ready to begin on the head of his fish, he made sure I saw him. When "Operation Eye" began, I turned my head away and he thought it was very funny. Some things I will try once but such things as fish eyes and octopus (which was served at camp), I turned down. Goats do not need to worry for their lives around me, either. I ordered goat meat once and that was enough.

After we had traveled some distance further, we stopped again at a restaurant for dessert. We were to choose a sweet to go with ice cream and what a problem that was! The Greeks certainly know how to make delectable sweets and decorate them beautifully. It made a very satisfying finish to a Greek meal.

It had been a wonderful day filled with unusual experiences. But my main purposes for visiting Greece—visiting Elpitha and her mother, and the orphanages I had helped, and seeing little Vasiliki—had been accomplished. I was ready and willing to start for home.

CHAPTER 8

Laughing Our Way Home

Early the next morning we packed all our luggage in the Volkswagen and began the long trek north through western Europe. I tell you, that little car was FULL! There was just room for the three of us to sit. My original misgivings about how three generations—Mr. Diavastes, a man you might say was in the prime of life; his teenage daughter, Ruth; and this retired schoolteacher—would get along traveling together were unfounded. We saw so many interesting things and found ourselves in so many ridiculous situations that we—at least Ruth and I— laughed much of the way to London.

We started across the Peloponnesus—the lower part of Greece which the Bible calls Achaia—and stopped at the ancient city of Corinth where the Apostle Paul preached so long ago. It took a great deal of energy to clamber over those old ruins and much watchfulness not to slip and fall. There were marble statues all around, most of them headless. Mr. Diavastes stood on a low wall back of one statue so just his head was visible above it and I took his picture. He looked so chic in his flowing marble robe!

It took nearly all day to cross the peninsula, driving along the Corinthian Gulf. We would board a ferryboat at Patrai on the western coast for Brindisi, Italy. It was a beautiful day for traveling.

There was a gypsy village not far from Patrai that

Mr. Diavastes wanted to visit. He knew a pastor who had been a gypsy boy in this village. He had been converted and interested people had helped him through Bible school. Now he was pastor of a growing church and Mr. Diavastes wanted to tell his Christian parents about their son.

There seemed to be many gypsies in Greece. We had passed several caravans of them as we were driving. Several little wagons pulled by horses were loaded with all ages of people and their belongings. I wanted a picture of them and one day when there was a man with us we stopped. Before I could take a picture several gypsies were at our car begging. The man gave them a coin and we made a quick exit.

The gypsies in this village had settled down in houses but the surroundings were very unkempt. As we neared the village it began to rain, and it poured heavily. It was difficult to find the right family as so many had the same name as this young man.

Mr. Diavastes got a gypsy boy to go along with him to help direct him. One could see youngsters hurrying to other homes to spread the news that there were strangers in their village. Several teenage boys got themselves a ringside seat in a big open door of a building near the car and watched us like hawks.

Mr. Diavastes finally found the family and went in the house but soon he came to the door and shook his head for Ruth and me not to come in. From the looks of the place we were happy not to have to. He had only planned to stay a short time but it began raining even harder and he had to stay in the house for some time—long enough to be offered refreshments. Finally the rain slowed down so he could come out and we were soon on our way, laughing over this very different experience.

At Patrai we made out our exit cards for Greece and entry cards for Italy, had lunch, and drove onto the ferry. In a way it was hard to leave Greece. Everyone had been so kind and had done so much for our pleasure. Farewell, Greece, there will always be a warm place in my heart for you. May there be better days ahead for you.

It was almost dark when we drove onto the ferry and we went directly to our staterooms. I had a room with a middle-aged Greek woman. I was glad she could speak a little English. I had to sleep "upstairs" but as the sea was quiet I wasn't in danger of falling out. There was so much loud talking by the crew that it was difficult to get to sleep.

The ship took us up the western coast of Greece, through the Ionian Sea. The next morning we made a stop at Corfu Island and crossed the Strait of Otranto up to Brindisi on the eastern side of the heel of the boot of Italy.

The boat was very crowded and it was difficult to find a seat. But the food was good, and I was glad for mealtime as one was sure of a seat for that long.

We had a time getting to our car when we landed. It had been parked at the back of the boat in a corner and the cars were parked so closely it was very difficult to get through them. It paid to be skinny.

There was a lot of red tape everyplace we went because of the car. Insurance and purchase papers had to be examined every time we crossed the border into another country. I was disappointed that the officials in some countries never looked at our passports, though. We would offer them and when they saw the U.S. covers they would just wave us on. I wished they had stamped them as the stamps would have made my passport more interesting.

It was six o'clock by the time we got off the boat and we had real difficulty finding a hotel in Brindisi for the night. We drove along a high wall on both sides of the street for a long distance. We didn't have an idea what might be behind the wall. Finally we came to a place where some people were on the street and inquired of some of them where we could find a hotel. After some difficulty, they seemed to understand what we wanted and directed us to a place called "Minerva" which seemed to be outside the city.

We drove for miles in the direction they pointed but didn't see any place we thought looked like Minerva. Soon we were out in the country where houses were far apart and it was getting dark. We finally saw a little village to the right of us and went over to inquire.

An American car was parked in front of one house and Mr. Diavastes lost no time getting over there. An American lady answered the door. She was the wife of an Air Force man stationed nearby at a large airbase. She drew a map to show us where Minerva was so we started out again and finally found it. But there was no room. It turned out to be a place we wouldn't have wanted to stay if there had been room.

There was nothing else to do but head back to Brindisi. At last we found rooms at the International Hotel and Ruth and I had to pay $10 for our room, the most we ever had to pay. It was so late we were glad for shelter at any price, but it turned out our price did not include a workable lock on our door. We piled all our luggage in front of the door, and felt that would discourage anyone from trying to break in. In spite of how serious it could have been, the sight of it gave us both the giggles as we got in bed.

We arose early the next morning and started across Italy for Naples, or Napoli, as they call it in Italy. While we were in Greece we had no language problems because both Ruth and her father could speak Greek. But after we left Greece our troubles began. It was often as good as a circus trying to get others to understand what we wanted. We tried to get information from gas stations on the way. Generally all the help we obtained was the direction in which they pointed. We would head in that direction and when we didn't find what we were looking for we would ask again—and go in the direction pointed. We generally toured the city before we found what we were looking for. I am sure we spent as much for gas trying to find locations in the cities as we did on the highways.

One day we stopped at a gas station and asked for directions. The answer came like a bullet, "Straight ahead!" We were so stunned to hear our own language spoken so perfectly when we were braced for another torrent of unintelligible sounds that all we could do was to stare at each other. Then we broke out laughing.

So many of the cities have very few traffic or stop signs and there seemed to be no speed limits. It was nerve-wracking—the driver was frantically trying to keep from running into others while at the same time trying to keep others from crashing into us. Just as frantically, we passengers were hunting street and road signs that didn't seem to exist. It was a relief when we reached the highway again.

The drive from Brindisi to Naples was beautiful. We saw so many vineyards and fruits of many kinds, including olive, almond, fig and citrus. The architecture of the houses was very strange—some houses looked like beehives with a pointed roof. The ground was stony. Stone fences separated all the fields and still the ground seemed almost covered with stones.

While trying to find a hotel we wandered down into the slum section of Naples. All of the city looked dirty. We saw a lot of garbage piled out on the streets. The tenements looked so poor. After touring most of the city in our usual direction-seeking way, we at last found a hotel and obtained rooms.

Since we still had several hours of the afternoon left, we decided to try to see Pompeii. We walked several blocks and then got on a train. We could see the mountain long before we reached it. The area of excavation was fenced in but we could see much of it from the fence. Just as we arrived, the gate closed and would not open again until 9 'clock in the morning.

Of course, it was a disappointment since we had gone to all the trouble and expense to get there. As we retraced our steps back to Naples, the other two were planning to try it again the next morning but I was hoping they wouldn't. It looked just like another ruins, the like of which we had already climbed over three times and I didn't feel it would be different enough to make the trip back to see.

We were on the last bus going back to Naples when we missed the place to get off. Rather than get even more mixed up, we stayed on the bus to the end of the line and came back with it. Then we misjudged our landmark and got off a couple stops too soon. We had a long walk through a big park to get back to our hotel. Ruth and I were so tired we could scarcely take another step. The whole situation seemed so ridiculous we started giggling again—and laughed a good share of the way back. I'm afraid her father was a bit disgusted with us, but I guess giggling at our predicament was better than griping.

In nearly all the places where we stayed at night the traffic subsided somewhat, but in Naples it was as bad at night as in the daytime. We were able to sleep very little. I was so tired the next morning I told them not to make the trip back to Pompeii for my sake. Ruth said she was too tired to go and as her father had been there before, we decided to move on to Rome. I reassured myself that if anyone asked me if I had been to Pompeii, I could say, "Oh, yes, I was at Pompeii," because I actually had been there. But no one ever asked me.

We reached Rome before noon and tried to locate some hotels listed in a guide book Mr. Diavastes had, *Europe on $5 a Day*. Many rooming houses and eating places were listed in it at modest prices. The book may be helpful if you can find the places. We couldn't.

The hotels we were looking for were near the big railroad terminal. We had driven and inquired, driven and inquired in our usual custom until we were exhausted. Finally he asked me to draw some railroad tracks, which I tried to do. With all the bumping over rough streets, I guess my drawing looked more like an abstract picture than railroad tracks. He showed it to the next person he asked for directions and Ruth and I almost exploded before he was through. I hope the man didn't think we were making fun of him for he did everything humanly possible to help us under the circumstances.

The conversation went something like this:

"Pardone, Senor, which way to the railroad station . . . terminal . . . stachio . . . train . . . choochoo?" as Mr. Diavastes showed him my drawing. I guess he thought that if one word did not get through, another might.

After several exchanges, Mr. Diavastes very graciously said, "Gracias, Senor," and from the tone I supposed he understood what the man had said. Then he turned to us and asked, "Did you get what he said?"

No, we certainly hadn't, so we got on the merry-go-round again. By keeping in the direction our informants pointed we finally reached our destination.

While in Rome we depended on buses, trains, and Shanks' horses, until the latter almost wore out. We took tours which took us through several large churches, traveled on the old Appian Way, saw the Colosseum, Circus Maximus, and went down into the Catacombs of St. Callixtus. It was a gruesome place. It made one realize something of the desperate times when people had to resort to such a place to worship God. I had a fresh feeling of thankfulness to God for freedom of worship.

The next day we visited St. Peter's Cathedral. What a huge place that is! We saw many of Michelangelo's marble statues. It is almost unbelievable how anyone can take a slab of cold marble and put so much life in it. We saw statues of saints, popes, historical and Biblical characters everywhere. The painted ceilings must have caused many stiff necks.

There were altars for worship all over the place and Mass was being said in several of them. They were off to one side of the huge building, I suppose so tourists could move around without disturbing the services. We saw many confessionals and a few people were confessing. If the priest was in the confessional, a red light showed. A sign over it indicated what language the priest spoke.

We saw a black statue of St. Peter and people were rubbing their hands over the feet and making signs of the cross. Many kissed his foot which had been rubbed so many times it had been almost rubbed away. We went down to a lower level where there were the crypts, the burial places of many popes. There were fresh flowers at the tomb of the late pope. A priest gave people flowers that had been first touched to the tombs.

We had been warned not to leave anything in our

car because of danger of theft, so we had taken all our luggage to our rooms. Early the next morning we had to lug everything back down and pack the car again, which was a big job. At this hotel we had to pay 10 lire every time we used the elevator, which was not quite 2¢ in our money. When we first arrived in Italy I cashed a travelers check for $20 and received 12,000 lire in exchange. That seemed like a lot of money to be carrying around.

We made very good time on the road and reached Milan by 9 o'clock. We stopped to see the famous Milan Cathedral. The outside looked like stone lace. The doors were covered with tooled copper figures of Bible characters and stories. They would have been beautiful if they had been cleaned and polished.

In dining places, we often ended up with food we could hardly eat. It was a problem many times for the waitresses to understand what we wanted. At one place where Ruth and I went we had such a time ordering that the waitress went to the kitchen and brought out three or four dishes and then pointed to the menu so we could know what foods were on the menu. Many times we would stop at a little grocery store to buy food and eat in the car.

The country of northern Italy was much different from the southern part. The architecture changed, too. The land became hilly and then mountainous until we had our first glimpse of the mighty Alps. I'll never forget my first sight of them! To think I was actually seeing the Alps that I had read about so often through the years was difficult to believe.

The word for the scenery was "immense" and worth the whole trip just to see it. I didn't like the hairpin turns and steep cliffs beside the roads and many of them had no safety rails. We went through numerous tunnels. When we reached the end of the long St. Bernard tunnel we had to show our passports at the Swiss border. It isn't a tunnel through the mountain but a road around the side with a roof over it and side railings. It extends for miles and seemed quite a marvel to me. We were told it was built this way for protection from snowslides in the winter.

We found a small chalet-type hotel in a tiny village of Liddes and took rooms for the night. The village was a charming place and the quiet was deeply appreciated after the bedlam and noise of the cities we had left behind. We had traveled thirteen hours from Rome that day.

We drove through the breadbasket section of the country to Bern and late afternoon reached Zurich

We sometimes bought food at a grocery store and enjoyed eating it along the way, as Ruth and her father are shown doing.

where we parked the car by the Rhine River and did a bit of shopping. We always looked for the lower-class hotels to stay. I do not care to stay in those high-class places when in a foreign country. They pattern after the West so much that it is almost like staying in an American hotel. One doesn't learn much about their customs that way. I want to know how the common people live. All except one hotel was very clean, and it wasn't too bad.

We could see a difference in the countryside as soon as we came into France. There were no longer the neat, tidy homes and clean waysides we had left behind in Switzerland and Liechtenstein. The country through France was so monotonous and uninteresting that I grew very tired and sleepy before we reached Paris.

We almost walked our legs off in Paris, visiting the Louvre Museum of Art, where we saw more pictures by the old masters, the original Mona Lisa, crown jewels, beautiful glasswares, and so many wonderful things. We thought we would go to the Eifel Tower and Triumphal Arch but it was farther away than it looked, so we gave up and sat in the park and watched people.

To reach our hotel we had to take a subway train. The car we boarded was so crowded with people we could scarcely breathe. Ruth and I thought we would be smart and get a seat by the door so we could get off quickly. What a mistake! We discovered it was the worst seat on the train. Elbows poked us at eye level and I was afraid my glasses would get broken so, somehow, I was able to put them in my purse. It was really amusing, but it seemed that Ruth and I were the only ones who thought so from the looks on some passengers' faces. We were so glad when we could get off.

The bathrooms in our hotel, as in most other places

in Europe, are called water closets. We discovered why. One was off the stair landing near our rooms and the facilities consisted of hole in the floor and a chain to pull for flushing. When the water was flushed it covered the floor. After the first time, one learned to step up on the door threshold. Our room faced an open well in the center of the building and many pigeons were flying around in it. Our windows had no screens and we were afraid they would get in our room, but they didn't.

Our next stop was Brussels, Belgium. Mr. Diavastes planned to leave the car there to be shipped back to the United States and from then on we would have to take care of all our bags and other luggage by hand. How I dreaded it. That evening we made three packages of extra things which we were going to mail home to cut down on the weight and number of pieces to handle. We planned to take them to the post office the next morning to mail. We were leaving the continent for London the next day.

We decided the next morning to take our luggage down to the office and leave it there until we came back from the post office. As the elevator was small we put part of the bags in and Ruth and I started down with it. Her father would wait until we were down and bring the elevator back up and take the rest of the bags down.

The plan was good, but before we could get out he signaled for the elevator to come up. It did, and when the doors opened, there we were! We told him he hadn't given us time to get out. Down we started again but before we reached the first floor someone on the second floor pushed the button to bring it up. There we were again!

Down we started the third time, but Mr. Diavastes thought we must certainly be out, so he pushed the button, and did we all feel silly to see each other again. I suppose people thought those women had never ridden in an elevator before.

We started down for the fourth time and were so excited and anxious to get out that we pushed the wrong button. Instead of stopping at the first floor, we landed on the ground floor. That meant we had to carry all of our luggage up to the first floor. We were laughing so hard we scarcely had the strength to carry it up the stairs.

We asked the hotel clerk for directions to the post office. Why she didn't tell us it was closed on Saturday, we will never know. We tried to find it but couldn't. A young fellow kindly took us with him for several blocks until we could see the building. When we arrived we learned the place was closed. Someone said the main post office might be open so we hired a taxi there only to learn it was closed also. The taxi driver overcharged us in the bargain. We hired another to take us back to the hotel as it was nearing train time. Instead of subtracting from our luggage, we just added three more packages.

I bought my ticket and when we were going through the gate Ruth discovered that she didn't have a return ticket. The conductor had evidently taken her return ticket by mistake when they first came to Europe. They had to buy another for her as no amount of talking would persuade the ticket agent she had had one. It would take two weeks for a refund to be obtained.

The trouble over the ticket made us late getting on the train and it was so crowded we could not find seats. Ruth and I had to park in the end of the baggage car where the conductor had his small office. Her father browsed up and down the coaches looking for vacant seats. At last he found some that would be vacant at the next stop. One of the companions in the compartment we found was an

African girl who had just graduated from a seven-year Engineering course in Prague and was going to London. She was very friendly and stayed with us until we parted in London. When we arrived at Oostend, Mr. Diavastes handed our large bags out the window to a porter waiting beside the train. It had been a rough ride.

The jam of people was terrific when our passports were checked for boarding the boat for Dover, England. When we were all on board it looked like a refugee ship leaving a disaster area. And we felt like it. The two top decks were covered with deck chairs so close it was almost impossible to move about. We were on the top deck with no protection. If an accident had happened we wouldn't have had a chance. How merciful God was to give us smooth sailing and no rain.

It was not a pleasant ride and when it came time to claim our luggage at the end of the trip, it was pure bedlam. Ruth and the African girl would hand pieces of ours over the heads of people and I would take care of it. When we were leaving the boat I noticed a carton of cigarettes in one of the bags I was carrying. As none of the three of us smoked, I supposed someone had put it in one of our bags by mistake, so I threw it out.

When I caught up with the African girl she looked at the bag and asked where her cigarettes were. Oh, my! I apologized and told her I would make it right. She said I looked so sad and for me not to worry. What made me sad was that it was cigarettes I had to replace. I went back to see if I could find them but someone else had probably picked them up.

This delay made us late boarding the train and all the seats were taken. Ruth and I had to again take refuge in the baggage car. So much baggage was put in the car there was almost no room to stand. The next car had "reserved" stickers on the windows but people were going in and so did we. It must have been reserved for a tour for when the guide saw some of us in the coach he was mad as a hornet. We couldn't understand him but the African girl could and she gave him a tongue lashing about his discourteous speech. They had a tongue battle for quite some time. He evidently understood English for she spoke in that language loudly enough for everyone to hear. It was quite entertaining.

We felt we had paid the same amount to ride as the tour, and very likely had paid more. But back to the baggage room we went.

Later we ventured to the door of the coach again and several fellows very courteously, with a big sweep of their arms, offered us their seats and they perched on the arms of the seats. And thus we rode into London.

CHAPTER 9

In England and Scotland!

We arrived at Victoria station about 8 o'clock. We had had very little breakfast—Europeans don't know what good breakfasts are, they were generally very thin affairs of rolls, jam and tea. And we'd had almost no lunch on the boat. Tired and hungry, we didn't know where we were going to stay for the night in London. Each of us bought four pieces of something to eat and shared it with each other, which helped.

Before he left the United States, Mr. Diavastes had tried to get reservations for us at the "House of Rest," a London missionary home, but they could not take us. He called from the train station to see if perchance there had been cancellations, but they still had no room. They told him to call the Foreign Missionary Club which sometimes took transients. He did, and they had some vacant rooms. He hired a taxi to take us there, and so ended the most difficult day of the trip.

This Christian club was like a haven of rest. It was very inexpensive, and we could get our meals there. There were also laundry facilities available which were most welcome by this time. About forty people were staying at the Club, and morning and evening prayers were conducted which we joined when we could.

The next day was Sunday and the colored fellow at

our table invited us to go to church with him. We went to the All Souls Anglican Church where the rector is the chaplain to Queen Elizabeth. A black man in bright clerical robes had charge of the service and for a time I thought he was the rector. They sang psalms and I don't know how they ever remembered the tune as there were no notes in the songbooks.

On the way to church we saw a Salvation Army band playing on the way to their citadel. We met some Christians from India who were also on their way to church. The woman had on a bright costume and there were two children. Our guide knew them and introduced us to them. We had to ride a long distance by bus to and from the church.

We had a very good dinner at the Club. It consisted of chicken, sausage, potatoes, peas, and gooseberry pie for dessert. The pie was delicious and I never saw such large berries. For breakfast we had cereal, boiled egg and tea. We hardly knew how to act with such good food offered to us. It was good to get water without asking for it, which was not true wherever we went on the Continent.

We were grateful for a good rest in the afternoon and in the evening we joined some others from the Club going to Westminster Chapel near Buckingham Palace. This was an independent evangelical church where Dr. Martyn Lloyd-Jones was a former pastor. It was a large and well attended church. A man from Cardiff, Wales was preaching and there was no liturgy in the service.

They had a strange custom, however, when beginning a song. The organist of the large pipe organ held the first note several counts longer than necessary, and with no song leader to direct, the people didn't all get on board at the same time. Everywhere I attended church in all my travels I noticed the songbooks had only words and no music.

They had no song leaders and the singing was nearly all in unison. Except in Korean churches, there was never any special music. Nevertheless, I always enjoyed the experience of attending church.

Even the weather while we were in London was cool and damp most of the time. Our room at the Club was never very warm. There was a gas heater on the wall and one could have some heat by inserting a coin in a slot. The building was an old one and the furniture was badly worn, but the Christian atmosphere made up for any inconvenience we may have experienced.

One morning during the prayer time a man from South Africa gave a wonderful prayer and he especially prayed for America. It was at the time of the awful publicity we had during the Democratic Convention. I thanked him after the meeting for praying for our country. He was almost in tears when he talked. His burden seemed to be that the fate of the world hung on the United States. If we went down all would be lost.

The following morning I had a chance to see something I had heard so much about—the changing of the guard at Buckingham Palace. We were at the palace about an hour and a half before the event to get a good vantage point, for thousands of people come to watch it every morning. We had a good spot, right at the front gate next to the fence. It is amazing the pageantry they go through just to exchange guards! The English certainly know how to put on a good show.

First, there was a parade of brilliantly uniformed horseguards. Then the band came, dressed in scarlet and black uniforms, followed by a large company of guards also dressed in scarlet uniforms and high bearskin hats that almost hid their eyes. As the band played they marched, countermarched, and trooped the colors. One guard led a large gray dog, which I thought was probably a mascot of the guards.

It was amusing to watch the sentries march back and forth in front of the palace. They walk as stiff as pokers to the end of the beat, then they stand and give a hard stomp with the right foot and then with the left. They pivot around in the opposite direction and really give a hard stomp with the right foot. They march back and repeat the performance at the other end of their beat. This is done over and over for a time, then they stand like statues in front of their sentry box for a time. When later we were viewing the sentries at Edinburgh Castle in Scotland, our guide showed us the depression the guards had made in the pavement from their marching. There was a deeper depression at the end where the harder stomps were made. We didn't see any of the royal family. Queen Elizabeth didn't invite us in for tea.

One afternoon we took a sight-seeing tour of London and saw many interesting places. We noticed statues of some of our great men in the parks and public places, but we saw nothing for George Washington.

Another day we visited the Tower of London, which is a place full of English history. We saw the crown jewels and the museum of ancient knight's armor and many artifacts of life there long ago. We were in the Bloody Tower and the room where Sir Walter Raleigh wrote his famous world history. I took a picture of Ruth as she was talking with one of the yoemen of the guard (called beefeaters).

A very unusual place, the famous wax museum, gave me a very strange feeling. It gave me a queer sensation to see a room full of people and not a sound coming from any of them. It almost looked like Judgment Day had come!

There were figures of people representing every

walk of life and from different parts of the world all down through history. Queen Elizabeth and Prince Philip held the center of the stage. Henry VIII and his six wives were there. Other members of the present royal family were in a group by themselves. Heads of countries, religious leaders throughout the centuries, military figures, musicians, artists, sportsmen—they were all there. Winston Churchill was seated at his easel painting, with an old straw hat on his head and wearing baggy pants. There were several historical groupings, one of which was very gruesome. Mary Queen of Scots had her head on the execution block with the executioner standing by with a white apron on and his axe ready for the fatal blow. That was almost too lifelike for me.

I crossed the Atlantic in almost half the time it took us to go by bus from London to Edinburgh. It was a twelve-hour ride and so tiring. The English countryside was very pretty and the patches of heather as we neared Scotland made one feel Scottish to see it. We saw flocks of sheep everywhere. We passed very few towns and the moors looked dark and lonely. They have much rain so the vegetation is very green.

When we arrived in Edinburgh at almost 8'oclock, we learned that a group of people were finding rooms for visitors because the Edinburgh Festival was on and many people needed lodging. We went to this agency and got there just in time as they closed after assigning us a place to stay in a private home. As tired as we all were, we were dismayed to find we had to take a bus quite some distance to the home. But the people were lovely and their home was clean and pleasant. They spoke English well so it wasn't difficult to talk with them.

After a good night's rest and the best breakfast we had had for many days, we took a conducted tour the next morning. We visited St. Giles Cathedral, or as our guide said, it should be the High Kirk of Scotland, as Presbyterians do not have cathedrals. Much of the history of Scotland is connected with this church. We were in Holyrood Palace where Queen Elizabeth stays when she is on state business in the country. We were in the rooms she occupies and also the room where knights receive their title. We saw some of the handwork made by the former Queen Mary.

Edinburgh is a beautiful city. We had such a lovely view of it from the Edinburgh Castle, which stands on a hill. We went through part of that building. The guard, wearing kilts, stood at the entrance gate like a statue and never recognized anyone. Mr. Diavastes found that out when he asked if we might take his picture. Since he didn't say we couldn't, we did.

Nearly all the chimneys on the houses have several small chimneys in them. Each chimney connects with a fireplace in the house because they do not have central heating. I thought how thankful I was for my furnace. Nearly all the houses are built with stone or brick and most of the houses in town are in long rows, joining each other. You can't "go around the house" there.

I was interested in the unusual signs we saw in Scotland and England and made note of some. I imagine there were some gems in other countries if I could have understood their languages. Here are some of them:

A pharmacist is a "chemical dispenser."
"No tipping" means no dumping.
"Give away" means to yield the right-of-way.
"A dust bin" is a garbage can.
A "poulterer" sells poultry.
A "purveyor of food" is a grocer.

A "confectionary purveyor" sells candy.
An "iron monger" sells articles made of iron.
"Fancy butcher" struck me as funny. I
wonder if he crochets fancy borders around
his steaks.
In the restaurants, "chipped potatoes" are
the same as shoestring potatoes for us.
"Dressed cabbage" is just plain old
boiled cabbage.

Scotland was interesting, but I was glad to be
heading back toward London. After the twelve-hour
bus ride we arrived in London early in the morning.
We slept most of that day, after we were able to get
into our room in the hotel which had been reserved
for us before we went to Scotland.

Ruth and her father took me to the air terminal the
next morning. I was GOING HOME! We said our
farewells at the terminal for they could not leave
until the next day. Mr. Diavastes and Ruth had been
wonderful traveling companions and had tried to
make everything as easy for me as they could. I will
never forget their willingness to take an older person
along on such a hard trip, not knowing how I would
stand it. Without their help and that of my friend
Elpitha, I could not have made the trip. I will feel
indebted to them for the rest of my life. My deepest
thanks to them and my wonderful Heavenly Father.

CHAPTER 10

Christmas in Free China

When I arrived home, I was so full of joy to be back safe and sound after eight tremendous weeks in Europe, I wouldn't have traded my old house for both Buckingham Palace and Holyrood. When I think of all I went through and the many things that happened during those eventful weeks, I marvel at all God did for me. So much could have happened, but God wonderfully protected, guided, and gave me strength for each day. The memories will keep me company as long as I live.

I settled down to rest and recuperate. Of course, as my body gained strength I was soon busy sewing again. I had to get the rest of those comforters done so I could send them to the orphanage in Thessaloniki to brighten those twenty beds of the dear Greek girls there.

People have always appreciated the comforters as these letters show. A superintendent wrote:

We received your nice eiderdowns and enthusiasm of the borders (orphans) was indescribable. Please accept the earnest thanks of the govern consultation and of the borders.

And another:

Everytime I look at your kind countenance in

the picture you sent us, and I see you bent over your loom working in behalf of my little orphan girls, I do admire and congratulate you with all my heart. We pray for you earnestly and ask the Lord to bless you richly and reward all your sacrifices, here, and a hundredfold in His heavenly kingdom.

The girls wrote:

We were so glad to receive your loving letter and your wonderful picture. Our spiritual mother read your letter to us and we enjoyed every single word of it very much. Your kind face touches us very much and your great love to us thrills our hearts to the depths. We are so thankful for the warm comforters you have sent us and as we feel so nice and warm in them we pray that you may feel the same in God's love and care. We appreciate this very much as we know it is done by your own hands.

Such expressions of appreciation made the time I spent sewing and praying for these dear children very worthwhile, and I praise God for the privilege of serving Him in this way.

During the following year (1969) I became interested in Chinese people and their country of Free China, Taiwan. Two deacons from my church were calling one evening on new visitors. They visited Dr. and Mrs. Yun Chung Sun, a young Chinese couple from Taiwan, and learned that Mrs. Sun was very lonely and homesick. She had been in the United States only two weeks and wanted desperately to have an American friend, one who would help her with the English language. She could speak enough English to converse, but she felt the need of more study.

One of the deacons, who knew of my interest and contacts with Oriental people, telephoned me that evening to ask if I would call on her. I was delighted for this opportunity to get acquainted with someone of another nationality. I visited her the next afternoon and thus began one of the most wonderful friendships I have ever had.

She and her husband were soon calling me their American Mother, and little six-year-old Homer called me his Grandma. Another little boy past two years of age soon began to realize he had a Grandma, too. When Homer had his sixth birthday, his mother told him he could invite four of his little friends over. When she asked him who he wanted, "Grandma" was the first one named.

Dr. and Mrs. Yun Chung Sun and another Chinese friend and I enjoyed seeing the Korean dress Ki Poong's wife in Korea made for me.

I don't think I could love children of my own more than I love this little family. They have done so many kind things for me and have been a real comfort. Mrs. Sun chose the name "Bonnie" for her American name, her Chinese name being, "Wan Ching."

Many times when Bonnie came to my home I would be sewing on garments to send to orphanages.

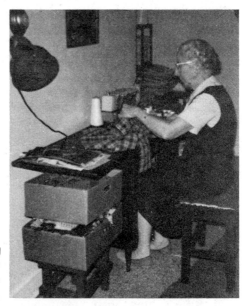

My sewing was usually done as a mass-production.

As she is a very tenderhearted person, a deep desire began to grow in her heart to do something to help this work. I suggested that she get in contact with some needy orphanage in Taiwan as there were many there.

Bonnie wrote to her former pastor in Taiching and asked him to recommend an orphanage. He gave her the address of the Christian Mountain Children's Home near Liu Kuei, in the mountains of southern Taiwan. Many of the children who live there are mountain children whose parents are so very poor they cannot support them. Through correspondence with the superintendent, Pastor Yang Shu, she learned about their great needs and began helping as she was able. Some months later circumstances led me to believe that God was directing my attention to this Home and I began making clothing for them.

The first box I sent was most gratefully received. Pastor Yang said it was the first new clothing they had ever gotten. They were saving it back to wear to "nice places," as he expressed it. Several more boxes were sent from time to time. Later he wrote that his Home was invited to some kind of meeting along with several other Homes and his children looked the nicest of all because they were wearing the clothing I had sent to them.

On April 3rd of 1972, I received the following letter from this pastor:

Dear Miss Ritchie:
   This is to invite you to come to Taiwan to preach the Gospel of Jesus in this mountain area and to help the work of our Home here. We are glad to be responsible for your living here. May God bless you.
       In His service,
       Yang Shu, Pastor

I was never so stunned over an invitation—and I was too shocked to think!

My first reaction was that it would not be possible for me to make another long trip, either physically or financially. The more I thought about it and discussed it with friends, however, the more I wondered if it could be God directing me. The thought kept going over in my mind, "Why not look into it, perhaps it isn't as impossible as it seems."

Finally I made an appointment to see my doctor and he saw no reason why I should not go. In fact, he thought it would be good for me. But there was still the cost to consider and I felt sure it would be more than I would dare to spend.

It so happened that Bonnie Sun was planning to go back to Taiwan to visit her parents in August and was going to fly on a Chinese charter plane from San Francisco at much reduced rates. The Chinese government runs these flights for the benefit of students studying in this country. I wondered if I might be able to get a seat on that plane and we could make the trip together. Bonnie said she would find out for me.

I left it in God's hands, and if the cost would be within my reach, I would consider it to be His directing. I soon learned I could ride on this plane and the round trip from Chicago would be $517. I was overwhelmed. Both of the reasons I felt I couldn't go were now swept away and I was sure I had my answer.

As my old passport had expired, I applied for a new one and also a visa. I took booster shots for the diseases I had had shots for on the first trip. I paid for my ticket on the charter plane from San Francisco to Taipei, and felt I was all set to go.

On July 5th I received word that I had to be a member of the student organization for six months in order to fly on this plane and be eligible for the discount. By the time I would go it would be only three months. I don't know why I was not informed of this regulation when I first contacted them. It was like someone had thrown a pitcher of cold water in my face. All I could think to say was, "Why, why?"

Then a voice seemed to say, "All things work together for good to them who love the Lord," and "God works in mysterious ways His wonders to perform."

After serious thinking I came to the conclusion that I would not have been able to stand the very humid weather they have over there during August, when Bonnie was going. I had decided on that time because I thought it would be nice to have company. In August, I learned, the humidity is great with temperatures as high as 110 and 115 degrees and much rain. Humidity is hard on me. As there were flights in December at Christmas time, I decided to plan my trip for that time. Their nicest weather comes at that time. It was satisfactory with the Home for me to go at Christmas, so I planned to go then for four weeks, instead of six as would have been necessary with the summer flight.

I learned a lesson through this experience about open and closed doors that I have never forgotten. My timing wasn't right so God closed the door, but He opened it again when the time would permit opportunities for joys I never could have had if my plans for summer had worked out. How much better it is to let God do the planning! He permitted me to begin preparations early enough so that when the time was right I would have the necessary number of months required for membership.

Bonnie went in August and she and the baby were both ill for several weeks. The heat was hard on both of them. How glad I was that I was not there to help complicate matters.

During the summer and fall I collected and packed gifts to send ahead to Taiwan and also to take with me to give the children at Christmas. That was indeed a happy experience.

At my request, I was informed that there were 61

children at the Home and learned the number in different age groups. I tried to have an article of clothing for each child and a little gift-wrapped package. I sent three large boxes on ahead early enough so they would be there in time for Christmas. There wasn't anything expensive, just such things as games, hairbrushes and combs, toothpaste and brushes, school supplies, small toys and such.

Several weeks before I went I thought I had better check to see what the present number of children was to be sure I had enough gifts. To my consternation I learned there were now 45 more children! Just imagine having your Christmas shopping "done" and discovering you still have 45 more gifts to get!

I had planned to take only one large piece of luggage, but now I would have to take another so I could carry at least part of that number of gifts and get the rest when I arrived in Taiwan.

I searched all over town looking for small items that would be suitable and would not take up too much room. A friend gave me some extra money which helped. Since all the packages I sent over from here had been gift wrapped, I had to do the same with what I took with me and would buy over there. So I took extra wrapping paper, tags to indicate age for the gift, and ribbons. I couldn't give part of them their gifts in the raw while others had pretty packages. I wonder what the inspectors thought when they looked in my bags.

The flight to Taiwan was pleasant but tiresome. My feet swelled badly from no exercise for such long stretches of time. My seatmates were two college students going home for Christmas. They were very interesting to talk with. One thought he would probably get married but he didn't know who the bride would be. Evidently the parents were arranging the wedding. If they wondered what this septuagenarian was doing on a students chartered plane, they were too polite to mention it.

I arrived in Taipei about 4:00 A.M. on the Friday before Christmas, which began Sunday evening. Bonnie, her family, Pastor Yang from the Home and the interpreter, Mr. Youeh, were at the airport to meet me. Bonnie and her sister-in-law took me shopping that afternoon and I bought some under-wear for boys and other small articles.

The map of Taiwan shows the long trip by railway from Taipei to Kaohsiung, near the Christian Mountain Children's Home.

I couldn't wrap any of the gifts that evening for they would take up too much room in my luggage that way.

Early Saturday morning, Mr. Youeh, Bonnie's sister Amy, and I took a fourth class train for Kaohsiung, a large city in the southern part of Taiwan near the Home. This meant traveling nearly the full length of the Island of Taiwan, and it took about six hours.

A fifth class train there would compare with our first class. In our fourth class train there were curtains and drapes at the windows which could be pulled to shut out bright sunlight. Small shelves at each window held two drinking glasses. After the train started a man came with a huge teakettle and poured boiling water in each glass. A uniformed hostess followed him with a plate of tea bags which she offered to each passenger. Since all water had to be boiled before drinking, this was a good way one could have a drink of water.

Pastor Yang, who had made the long trip back home Friday night, met us at the depot and had a taxi take us to the Home, which was another one-and-a-half hour ride. We arrived late Saturday afternoon at the Home.

The next evening was Christmas Eve, and still none of those 45 presents were ready. I had been asked to be one of the speakers at the Sunday morning church service, so I had to prepare, and we were to be at the Home for dinner Sunday noon and spend the afternoon there. Then it would be Christmas Eve! I don't think I was ever in such a mental stew as I was over those unwrapped gifts.

We had supper at the Home Saturday night and afterwards I was so anxious to get to my hotel room in Liu Kuei, the small village near the Home. But the dear polite people didn't want to rush me. Little did they realize what all I had to do yet that evening. My nerves were as tense as a fiddle string.

When we finally went to the village, we stopped at a market and I ordered enough oranges for each child to have one and also some mixed candy. I let Bonnie's sister Amy share my hotel room and she helped me get the gifts ready. How I did appreciate her help. We worked for a couple of hours until I was getting so nervous I wasn't putting the right things in the bags so we quit for the night.

The next morning I was awakened by a rooster concert. Nearly everyone has a few chickens. It did more to relax my nerves than pills could have done. There were solos, duets, quartets and unison crowing. I think every rooster in that area made a contribution to the concert. The tenor part must have been reserved for an old patriarch near the hotel. What gusto he put into his rendition—he pulled out all the stops. I had never heard anything so hilarious and I laid there and laughed until I suppose Amy thought I was crazy.

The Bible says that a merry heart doeth good like a medicine and it was surely true that morning. Amy had to leave early to go back home in Taipei, so I finished the gifts. I really felt relaxed.

Then I went to the home of Mr. Youeh, the interpreter, for breakfast. All of my meals were taken at the Youeh home while I was at Liu Kwei, except when I was at the Home at mealtime. The Youeh home was about two blocks from the hotel.

Mr. Youeh had been in the medical corps in the army and had a small clinic in his house for the poor people of his area who could not afford the services of a physician. They lived on the first floor of the church building, the auditorium being on the second floor. Their rooms were rent free for taking care of the building and doing janitor work. Their fur-

While I was in Taiwan, Mr. Youeh was my interpreter. I often ate with the Youeh family, shown here.

nishings were very meager and the floors were cement, but everything was clean and the food was carefully prepared and served. Very few homes of the poorer class have many comforts as we consider them.

Mrs. Youeh could not speak English which made it difficult to visit with her. During the time I was there we did have some lively games of badminton after I improved enough to be able to hit something besides thin air. She would often lay her head on her hands and motion to a chair as an invitation for me to rest. I always shook my head no.

They all thought I should be resting a great deal and should take naps. When a woman reaches 70 years over there she is not expected to do much and is supposed to rest a lot. They just couldn't understand why I didn't rest more. They often remarked about how young I looked at my age. I guess I was quite a conversation piece. I suppose they would not have been surprised to have seen me hobble off the plane leaning on a cane.

To ask someone their age is considered quite proper to the Chinese. So, if anyone is at all squeamish about telling their age, they should not go to Taiwan. I never could understand why so many people guard their age like it is a military secret. To grow old is neither illegal nor immoral. It is a natural process that no one has been able to stop. It is possible for minds to be young at 80, 90, or even older. As long as the brain functions normally, the real "you" can still be young. We grow old when we lose our zest for living.

I think Mrs. Youeh was ready to quit the game several times before I was. I thought, "Young lady, if anyone hollers 'Uncle,' it is going to be you." I felt it was the only way I could impress on them that I didn't go over there to rest half the time—it would have been cheaper resting at home.

On Sunday morning I was one of the speakers at the morning service in the church in Liu Kwei. Dr. Quick, an American missionary who helps the national pastors, was there and another young man who was on a trip to many Asian countries taking movies with a missionary emphasis. After the service Dr. Quick took us out to the orphanage for dinner.

The only entrance into the Home grounds is by way of a swinging footbridge. How I dreaded it each time. Weeks before I went, they had sent me slides showing some of the children crossing on it. I wrote and asked if that was the only entrance to the orphanage and they didn't answer my question, so I figured it was.

The footbridge was 130 feet long and it seemed like an endless distance to walk on something that trembled. It crossed a wide river but the water was low, actually bare in places. But that didn't help my feelings. The riverbed was full of stones, certainly not a good landing place. The children run over the footbridge easily and one boy just sails over it on a motorcycle. It almost made my heart stop beating to see him. There is a cable on each side and coarse fencing along the bridge, but it still looks dangerous.

I found it was easier crossing at night with a flashlight, since I couldn't see all that big empty space around me. The first time I crossed it, Mrs. Yang met me halfway and held onto my arm. I never tried it alone—someone always held my arm and sometimes there was one on each side.

When we arrived at the Home we discovered there was a large group of Junior College students there having a Christmas party for the children. I don't know who had the most fun—the students or the children. Some of the older boys could speak English and I began talking to several. Soon a crowd was around me. It didn't take long for them to begin the important business of finding out how old I was. I made them guess so they began at 40. I kept saying, "Too young," and as their guesses kept getting higher their eyes bugged out farther and farther. When they reached 75 I called it quits with 73. They were amazed. The next matter of business on the agenda was for them to have a picture taken with me.

A news reporter of one of the largest daily newspapers in Taiwan was there that day. Someone told him about me being there, and about my work. He was interested at once and wanted an interview. He said it was something everyone should know. The time for the interview was set for early in the evening.

Two members of the college faculty were there with

the students. They and the reporter were really striking in their appearance. All three Chinese men had coal black hair, wore dark suits, white shirts and black ties, hair neatly trimmed, and were clean-shaven. They looked very impressive.

Dinner was served outdoors in a kind of arbor. There were a number of round tables seating about ten people. I was asked to sit with the dignitaries, and they all participated in giving me a lesson on the art of eating with chopsticks. But, alas, I just could not acquire the Chinese technique any better than I could the Korean. It looks so simple when they use chopsticks and so difficult when I try it.

Dr. Quick took me to the hotel to rest awhile before the Christmas program in the evening. I wasn't tired, even though I had to cross that frightening footbridge.

When we went back to the Home at about 5:30, some boys carried the several bags of gifts across the footbridge for me. Supper was served in the guest house, but I was still so full from dinner that I couldn't eat any more and they couldn't understand why. It is simply amazing how much food Chinese people can eat and yet they do not look fat. I cannot recall seeing a really fat person all the time I was in Taiwan.

The reporter came and we had the interview and he took my picture. I put all the presents I had brought on some long tables by the side of the room in the guest house. The three large boxes I had sent in October were brought in.

Pastor Yang had wanted to keep the boxes un-opened for me. He said I would open them and give the gifts to the children. But unfortunately, the boxes had been opened at Customs and a few of the gift-wrapped packages had been torn open. One of the boxes was messed up quite badly. But when every-thing was all spread out, it was quite a sight!

The boys carried my bags over the 130-foot long
swinging footbridge. I dreaded each time I had
to cross it.

The children came in and watched television for a
time. The orphanage had been given a television by
a Taiwan company. Later the children sang carols
and the pastor gave a talk. Then I was asked to speak.
The reporter took a picture of me when I presented
Pastor Yang a check for $150 from our Junior
Church and staff in Midland. The children had saved
their church collections for nearly six months for me
to take to the orphanage in Taiwan.

The second part of the program was outside as it
was warm weather. A white-robed choir sang
Christmas carols. Then Santa came and the pastor
interpreted for him. It must have been very funny for
there was a great deal of laughter.

The oranges and other treats were distributed and then the children lined up to receive my gifts. I think each child thanked me. They looked so happy. I told them there was something in each package which they couldn't see—my love for them.

When I returned to the hotel that evening the boys wouldn't let anyone else carry my bags over the trembling bridge. They acted as though it was an honor to do it.

Mrs. Youeh went with me up to my room on the third floor at the hotel. It was frustrating, for neither of us could talk to the other, so she soon left. About midnight the children went caroling and came to the hotel to sing for me. I discovered that it is the custom to treat the carolers as we do at Halloween. As I wasn't prepared for this, Mr. Youeh gave me some candy from the Home to give them. Dear Mrs. Youeh went up to my room with me again. It probably was her way of being polite.

Christmas morning Mr. Youeh had my breakfast sent up to my room. It consisted of FIVE boiled eggs, FOUR large oranges, THREE rolls, and a bottle of something to drink that looked a little like milk. It had a peculiar taste. As I didn't know how it was supposed to taste, it could have been spoiled. I had a sick stomach the next day which I believe resulted from it.

I was astonished over the amount of food. I never eat more than one egg at a meal unless several are scrambled and I don't know where one leaves off and another begins. I ate one egg and kept one for evening lunch and gave the rest back.

I had trouble in the food department all the time I was in Taiwan. Plates would be heaped with food and there was always a large helping of rice. There would be several platters filled with combinations of meats and vegetables. Everything was cut up into

123

bite size pieces so they can be eaten with chop sticks. There was always a small bowl of some kind of thin soup. Some foods tasted very flat to one used to salting food. I noticed it most in the soup, eggs and chicken. Rice was often served in separate bowls and bites of other foods were put in the bowl and eaten with the rice.

After I had begun to make some inroad on the food on my plate, others at the table would begin to fill it up again—this one putting on a spoonful of one kind of food, another with something else, and then would come special tidbits from someone's chop sticks. I would protest vigorously that I couldn't eat so much, but it fell on deaf ears. I guess they thought I was just being polite.

It was explained to me that the thinking back of this custom is that the guest is too polite to ask for a second helping, so the rest take the initiative and give it to him. I felt that it was their generous hospitality that prompted this, but what do you do when your capacity won't accommodate it? I am a very small eater and do not eat as much as most people do. When I couldn't clean up my plate, I felt they thought I didn't like their cooking. I know Mrs. Youeh and others worried about cooking for me and I was sorry about that.

I had a chance to visit a number of different types of schools. I saw both the schools at Liu Kwei and met the principals and some of the teachers. One was a Primary school and the other a Junior High. I met the English teacher and the poor fellow had so much trouble speaking English I had to wonder how he could teach it. I was told that good English teachers were difficult to find, and was asked several times to come over and teach it.

The first thing in the morning, all the children gather on the playground and stand in formation at attention. They are given instructions for the day over a loudspeaker. They stand with their hands behind their back. All wear uniforms and the primary children all wear orange colored caps and hats and khaki colored suits. Older students wear broad-brimmed hats. All students carry khaki colored book bags as they have to take all of their books and school materials home each night. It looked like they also have Safety Patrols.

There was no hallway in the center of the buildings as we have, the classrooms on either side. All the rooms open outside and a long, covered walkway runs the length of the building. I walked past many classrooms and looked in through open doors and saw the students working. There was no fooling around anywhere I looked. Everyone worked like his or her life depended on doing a good job. I was told the pressures on students are terrific. The entrance exams to enter college are very difficult and only the top 20 percent are allowed to enter.

They are plagued with the problem of not having enough schools. Their aim is to give the best chances to those who are the best prepared. Those who are not accepted for college may enter a trade or vocational school. Suicide is common among those who fail for they feel they have let their family down and have lost face, a most distressing situation for Orientals. I felt very sorry for them.

Pastor Yang, Mr. Youeh, and Jack Hu, a young man who manages the Christian book store in Kaohsiung, took me sightseeing. We visited the Provincial Teacher's College and the president took us through the lovely, four-story, well-equipped library. We went to the famous Chen Ching Lake.

My guides contacted a medical professor whom they knew and he took us through the medical school and hospital. We met the president of the college, considered by many the best surgeon on the Island. We visited the lab, a classroom, a hospital ward, saw a budding dentist practicing on a patient, and saw the specimen cases.

The last place was rather gruesome. They had a glass jar containing 600 worms about two inches long taken from a mountain boy's stomach. That was just one-third of the total number found—1,800 in all—and the boy recovered. Many mountain people have worms as the water and food are contaminated.

We saw other schools, but the most beautiful of all was the Ming Dow Middle School at Taichung. It is large, with many buildings built by some wealthy Chinese businessmen. It took a half day to go through part of the buildings. They had 7,000 students, and half were night students—they also have classes from 6 to 10 P.M. Many students work in factories during the day and one has to wonder when they find time for rest, study or recreation.

In the English department, I had a nice chat with the teachers. They seemed glad to speak to an English-speaking person. Two of them were our guides. One dear girl put her arm through mine all the time. I had fun in a beginning English class of seventh graders. The teachers tried to get the children to talk to me but most of them were afraid to try it.

I had a wonderful opportunity to visit orphanages, hospitals, and polio homes. There are several organizations of worldwide fame that are doing marvelous work in these needy areas. World Vision, Mustard Seed, Evangelize China Fellowship, Norwegian groups, and Baptists are a few of those doing a great work in these needy places on the Island.

I was deeply impressed with the Mustard Seed Orphanages. These and many other kinds of rescue work have been founded by Mrs. Lillian Dixon, whose headquarters is in Taipei. I had the pleasure of meeting her in her office and felt it was an honor to shake her hand. Later I read the story about the official who questioned her ability to accomplish her dream, likening it to trying to drain the sea with a bucket. Her reply: "Well, since I am a Christian, I must take out my bucketful." When I heard that, I was determined to do all I could to take out my little bucketful to help life's unfortunates.

I think Mrs. Dixon's Mustard Seed Homes—about seventy different types of Homes all over the Island—were the nicest I saw. The houses were built of bright red brick, and the green grass around each house made them look so "homey." There were curtains at the windows, nice pictures on the walls, a fireplace in every room with a cheery fire (the weather was chilly), and the floors were tiled. The children were very well dressed. Many of them wore nice knitted suits and other good materials. It looked like they might have been dressed up for Christmas. It is almost overwhelming what one determined woman has been able to accomplish. She must have a faith that can move mountains. She never felt any project was too large for her—and God—to accomplish.

I also visited one of the underprivileged orphanages at Pingtung under the supervision of a dear elderly Christian Chinese lady. Only about half of her orphans were sponsored, so she lives by faith from day to day for her needs to be supplied. She did a great work on the mainland of China before being driven out. I spent part of a day and had dinner with her and my heart was deeply touched. I promised to send her some clothes, and a big smile lighted up her wrinkled face.

The polio homes were sad places. To see children

by the dozens hobbling around with braces and crutches when they should be running freely, touches one's heart. A Norwegian missionary, Mrs. Tjersland, took us to see the leprosarium in Kaohsiung which her husband had started. We saw some pitiful cases. She showed us some very beautiful embroidery work that a leper with only stubs of fingers had made. I was told that the handwork is disinfected so there is no danger of contracting the disease. I bought a beautiful luncheon cloth and napkins, and it is so perfect it almost makes me ashamed of my work done with normal fingers.

Pastor Yang Shu and his Home, the one I had come to Taiwan especially to visit, seemed to be known all over the Island. He had been honored three years in a row by the government for his work with the Mountain People, said to be the poorest people on the Island. It is wonderful how God has taken care of the children in his Home. No child had ever needed an operation, none had died, none had ever fallen into the river from the swinging bridge, and there had not been one case of snake bite when there are five kinds of poisonous snakes in the area— other children in the locality had been bitten. Needs of this Home are great.

I was treated on all these trips as if I were a piece of delicate china, but I often wished another woman could have been along. One afternoon I had three men as guides and the next day there were four. It seemed as though nothing was too good for me. I had to protest in order to carry my handbag. I'm like Linus and his security blanket in the "Peanuts" cartoon—I have to have something to hang on to.

I felt unworthy of so much effort on their part. I didn't feel I had done enough to earn so much attention. The fact that I was interested in seeing the people and getting acquainted with them instead of just seeing beautiful places seemed to warm their hearts. Three of the largest daily papers carried stories of my visit and one of them mentioned this in its report.

I am quoting a translation of this news story. I cannot refrain from making some corrections, however. All three reports contained these same errors. I do not know whether the reporters were so anxious to make a good story that they filled in parts they thought could be true or that would make a better story, or the problems were the result of not understanding the foreign language. I guess reporters are the same the world over. I do appreciate the spirit back of these stories as they were meant to express gratitude and happiness over my visit to them.

Dedicated life to serve others
thousands of miles away
here in Taiwan.
To keep company to the orphans
and comforting the sick,
Miss E. Ritchie explicating real love.
Taiwan News 11th Jan. 1973

Miss R. Ritchie, a 75 years old (*should be 73*) kind and loving-hearted lady from Michigan of the U.S., who is willing to serve people no matter what their nationality, age, and race they are, came to our Island on Dec. the 20th. During all these days she gave all her time to accompany orphans and comfort the sick. She will return to the U.S. on Jan. 17th, but she surely will leave here many inspiring memories to us.

Miss Ritchie's home is Michigan USA. She

---

had served in the work of teaching for 36 years, and has been retired 12 years now. She has some money from her retirement pension and also some from her well to do family. (*The last part of the above sentence is incorrect.*) After her retirement she could not settle down until she decided to serve orphans, sick, disabled, and old folks with her loving heart.

Miss R. adopted (*should be "sponsored"*) 5 orphans and supporting two adults (*adult support an error*). Beside the one she is supporting in Liu-Kwei orphanage, there is one in Greece, one in India, two in Korea, and there are two adults in special needs (*no adult support*).

It has been told she did so many of this kind of work, she even cannot remember all of them.

In this trip to come to the Republic of China, mainly to see some of the orphans, and at the same time she wants to meet and see us hard working and steadfast Chinese people. She was a teacher, so she understands the great spirit of Chinese people and the greatness of Chinese culture.

She arrived in Taipei Dec. the 20th and immediately accompanied by the Superintendent of the Liu-Kwei Orphanage for the Mountain People and went to their orphanage. She spent Christmas with the children in the orphanage.

Miss R. bought every child a suit of clothes and in addition gave them 6000 NT (*US $150 from Junior Church in Midland; I did not give each child a suit of clothes but tried to have some article of clothing for each—a dress, shirt, scarf or pajamas*) for Christmas gifts. After Christmas she went to Faith, Hope, Love Orphanage (*a new one I am adding to my sewing project*), Ping Tung Home for the Disabled, Home for

Polio children, and visited hospitals and comforted sick people. She went also to the Kaohsiung Leprosy Hospital, to serve those who are sick.

Jan. 9th she will leave here and go to the central part of the Island and visit more orphanages in that area also to visit the leper colony.

She will go back to the USA on the 17th and temporarily leave the friends here and she hopes she can come back during her lifetime.

There are foreigners who come to Taiwan just as tourists, visiting beautiful places; but Miss R. with a loving heart, disregarded the tiredness of the long distance travel. She has dedicated all her life to serving other people. She has really given many kindness and inspiration to the Chinese friends.

We wish Miss. R. will have a nice trip back to the USA and also hope that God will take care of her.

One paragraph from one of the other news reports is worth quoting here: "Miss Ritchie can't speak too much Chinese because of language difficulties. When she plays around with the children she often found it hard to express her feelings. At first the orphans felt strange toward this blond-haired and blue-eyed American and don't dare to get too close to her, but after two days this old Miss became the most welcome guest of the orphanage."

The hospitality of Chinese people is tremendous. Let them know you do not feel yourself above them and they open up the floodgates of their wonderful hospitality until you are nearly drowned with love. There were times I felt as though I was going down for the third time.

I have always had a great respect for that little bastion of freedom in the center of turmoil, and since I have been there it has grown tremendously. How tenaciously they are hanging on to their freedom. Policemen are everywhere. When a train comes in, several officers take their places and patrol two by two. An enemy who wants to take them by surprise will have to be very clever. Films brought into the country are censored before they can be shown in an effort to keep out subversive propaganda and X-rated movies. I didn't hear about any demonstrations against the regulations. The people seemed to appreciate the discipline that accompanies their freedom—knowing that freedom without discipline can only result in anarchy.

CHAPTER 11

I Will Never Forget You, Little Taiwan

Many amusing things happened during my time in Taiwan. Pastor Yang and Mr. Youeh took me up in the mountains to visit a grade school one day. It was quite a distance away and by the time we arrived they were dismissing school. I doubt if the children had ever seen an American before, the way they all stared at me. I don't suppose an elephant, if it had happened upon the school ground, could have caused more curiosity.

We looked around awhile and then went to wait for a bus to take us back to Liu Kwei. As there would be a forty-five minute wait, Pastor Yang went to one of the houses nearby and asked for a chair for me to sit on. A young mother came out of a house with a baby strapped to her back. I had been wanting a picture of this custom and thought this was an ideal chance to get it. But when the lady saw me with my camera, she hurried into the house and soon came back with the baby all dressed up in a nice knitted outfit, ready to pose for a picture. That wasn't the kind of picture I wanted, but I took one anyway.

As we waited, about a half dozen little boys put on a show climbing trees and then came over and stared at me. Next, a flock of turkeys put in their appearance and began milling around us. One of the boys picked up one of the gobblers almost as large as he.

It was such a funny sight seeing him struggle so hard that I took his picture.

Pastor Yang thought it would be funnier if each boy had a gobbler and the boys were most happy to oblige. Finally, there were four old gobblers trying their best to get away from four determined boys. Then the realization came over Mr. Youeh that I hadn't been in any of the pictures, and that wouldn't do. So the boys retrieved the sputtering turkeys again, which really offended the old gobblers' dignity. When the poor old birds were allowed to depart they hashed over that humiliating experience all the way to the woods. All of this commotion brought out the adults from the houses to see the show. They all seemed to enjoy it as much as we did.

I had to be in a picture with the boys and sputtering turkeys.

There are some excellent roads and streets in Taiwan but they haven't reached out much into the byways yet. Many of the roads were rough and stony, especially those up into the mountains. It almost makes me shiver yet when I think of some of the roads we traveled in the mountains. They were crooked and steep, with sharp turns and no guardrails for protection. I never saw roads that gave me so much motivation for prayer as those.

The bus jolted from side to side so much of the time that I felt all shook up by the time we reached our destination. But the scenery along the way was fascinating. Farmers in Taiwan certainly know how to make plants grow. I have never seen more luxuriant vegetation. Every available bit of earth was planted and the fields were all so free from weeds.

I felt sorry for the women who were in the fields all day working so hard. Then they would walk home in the late afternoon carrying a yoke over their shoulders, with a basket at each end filled with sugar cane, roots, vegetables, or wood. I saw one poor woman with such a large load of wood she almost staggered when she put it down.

They raise one kind of sugar cane that can be peeled and eaten raw. I often passed children and adults who were eating a stick of it much like we eat stick candy.

As the bus went through a small village one could see all kinds of manufacturing going on in the little shops and often on the sidewalk. One man was upholstering furniture and another was making furniture on the street. The whole store front rolls up during the day and pulls down at night. There is no windowshopping there at night after the store closes, but as it is usually 10:00 o'clock or later, probably no one would be interested.

There are so many food stands on the sidewalks. Food is served everywhere. Many food servers have small tables about the size of a card table on which they have all their supplies. Sometimes steaming kettles of hot food and serving bowls are moved on carts through the streets and stop when they find a customer.

Food is seldom covered. I used to watch the meat vendor in the morning when I was at the little hotel in Liu Kwei. He had fresh meat in an uncovered box on the back of his bicycle, along with a scale for weighing. Customers would come up and pick out the piece of meat they wanted from the box. Then, holding it in his hands, the vendor would weigh it and put it in a bag. He would handle money and then wait on the next customer.

Many homes in the small villages were built out almost even with the street or sidewalk. I had to wonder how people could see to work, there were so few windows. Sewers were open and boards were put over them in front of houses so people could walk over them to the street. I noticed that sewers were often used as toilets.

I saw women washing clothes in the irrigation ditches and in pools of water left in the rivers that were nearly dry. It was surprising how clean the clothes looked having been laundered under such great difficulties. I saw no clotheslines such as we use. Instead, women used bamboo poles, running them through the arms of shirts and one leg of the pants. I saw clothes drying in front of nearly every home we passed.

Children were everywhere. Women carried their babies on their backs in a kind of sack made from a blanket, tied in front—which left both hands free. Very few people have automobiles, but nearly all have motorcycles and entire families can be seen riding on them. I spent many minutes watching Free China go by my little hotel. Children going to school, food vendors, business people, trucks, people on bicycles, motorcycles, and men and women carrying heavy yokes filled with almost anything.

My room in the hotel was a tiny one, and I had just enough space to get around in it. There was a private bathroom, but I never had hot water. A large thermos jug was always kept filled with hot water, and there were cups for tea. A spitoon in my room made a good waste basket.

When the main light was turned off at night, a night light came on. The last couple days I had company—two salamanders which skittered over the walls. I tried to scare them away but they wouldn't leave. I wasn't afraid of them, but I didn't like the idea of salamanders exploring my bed at night. They were good little "sallys," though, and didn't bother me. The bedding consisted of two pillows and a sheet, and a thick downy comforter to cover up with. It was all very clean.

I had fun with the three children who belonged to the lady hotel manager. No one there seemed to know any English, so I began working with the children. And how they loved it! Their faces would light up when they saw me coming. We worked on words like *mouth, eyes, hair, hands, feet,* and *teeth.* They never forgot *teeth* and would open their mouths and show their teeth while saying the name.

I had one terrifying experience. One morning the interpreter and I left early for a trip up into the mountains to see a school where Pastor Yang teaches to help support his Home. I had heard about it and thought I would like to see the place, and we would also see an aborigine settlement. The road was rough and steep and frightening as the bus rounded curve after curve. When we were nearly to the aborigine settlement, we came to a roadblock across from a government building.

Mr. Youeh went inside and was gone so long I wondered what was wrong. After a time the officer in charge came out and motioned for me to get off the bus. I went into the office and showed him my passport and visa. He didn't say anything to me but I could see that he and Mr. Youeh were very angry about something. Mr. Youeh was talking on the phone and trying to get the officials to understand something. I couldn't understand what was wrong, but knew that whatever it was it seemed to concern me. I wondered what in the world I had done.

I went out and boarded the bus and in a short time I was asked to get off again. Then Mr. Youeh got on the bus and tried to get the passengers to understand something—and a great clamor arose. Chinese often sound angry when they are not, so when they are really angry it is something to hear—unless you are the subject of their wrath.

We must have been held up for half an hour and a number of young people left the bus and were standing around. I asked a young fellow what was wrong. Fortunately he could speak English and he told me I was supposed to have a pass to go up into the mountains and I didn't have one. So, it was what I hadn't done that was causing the disturbance. I felt terrible and wondered why my interpreter hadn't taken care of that business.

It seemed that one woman was causing all the trouble. I guess the officer would have allowed me to go through but she had raised such a rumpus he was afraid she would report him and he would lose his job. She didn't even want me up there with a pass! I think what made Mr. Youeh so angry was that his church had helped this woman's family and it made him lose his temper for her to act that way about someone who had come to help the people of Taiwan. He knew three of the four officers who rotate on guard duty and it happened that the fourth, who did not know him, was on duty that day. I later learned that passes are necessary to protect the mountain people from those who would take advantage of them.

Finally, we were told we could take the next bus, which came soon and we at last arrived in the mountain village. The main street into this village was most difficult to walk on as it was so rough and rocky. The housing was very poor. When we arrived, the students were eating their noon meal in heartbreaking surroundings. I never saw such a pitiful school building in my life! It looked as though a fire had gone through it. There were no electric lights and on a cloudy day, as it was then, I don't see how those children could see to read the tiny characters of their language.

Inside, the walls were dingy and not a pretty thing was in sight. Many of these precious children walk for two hours or more over steep mountain trails to come to this school, they are so eager to learn. I had to think of the beautiful learning palaces we have in America and of all the vandalism that happens to them. May God have mercy on us.

The government pays the teachers' salaries but it is up to the community to supply the equipment— and many communities are too poor to do it. Anyone willing to go to a place like that to help and teach is certainly dedicated. No wonder Pastor Yang has received several citations from the government for his work with these people. There were two other men teachers there who seemed like nice fellows.

The last night I was at Pastor Yang's Home they had a farewell supper for me. Afterwards a number of the older children came in the building and acted as though they hated to see me leave. When we left for Liu Kwei, two of the older girls took hold of my arms and helped me across the swinging bridge. They hung on as if they didn't want me to go. A taxi was waiting for me on the other side of the bridge, and as it pulled away, it was a sad time for me, too.

When it came time for me to leave Liu Kwei, Mrs. Yang brought twelve-year-old Joe with her to the bus terminal to see me off. I had been sponsoring Joe at Pastor Yang's Home for some time. Whenever he saw me, he would be all smiles. I had a picture of us taken together and I sent him one after I returned home. An enlargement was made for him and I was told later by letter that he would hurry home after school and go into the room where the picture was hanging and look at it. Oh, if only everyone who is able would take one of these dear love-hungry children to sponsor, how happy those two people would be—the sponsor and the child.

As we stood at the bus terminal there were tears in Joe's eyes and when he thought no one was looking, he wiped them away with the back of his hand. He is all alone in the world, and now the only one who loved him in a special way was leaving and likely would never come back. Mrs. Yang was in tears and so was I. I felt an awful tug at my heart and a piece broke off and will always be back there.

Mr. Youeh accompanied me on the eight-hour trip north to Taipei, and when we arrived at Bonnie's home we learned she was ill at her husband's parents' home. Circumstances were such that I couldn't stay at either place. Mr. Youeh did some telephoning and found a home on the Baptist Theological Seminary compound that would take me in. I found the Changs to be delightful people. He was head of the music department and his wife was involved in teaching English. They had two fine, well-behaved teenagers at home and one at a boarding school. Mr. Chang's father had been a pastor on mainland China and he had no way of knowing where his father was or if he was alive.

Mr. Chang had studied in the United States, and he said the people there had been so good to him he was delighted to have an opportunity to return those kindnesses by helping me. My stay in the Chang's home was most pleasant. One evening we had a little concert—the son and daughter playing violins, Mr. Chang the cello, and me at the piano.

Mr. Chang's wife, Jean, was to have been my interpreter and guide, but shortly after I came her mother fell, broke her hip, and had to have an operation—so Jean was at the hospital much of the time. On the Sunday before I left Taiwan, the Hogues, American missionaries who lived next door, had me move over to their home.

I went with the Hogues to their church on Sunday morning and was in Mrs. Hogue's Sunday School class. After the lesson she asked me to tell the ladies about my work. After dismissal one lady wanted her grandmother to hear the story, so it was decided that I would speak that evening at the Training Union period. When I arrived at church that evening, three tape recorders were set up to tape the service. Many American servicemen and businessmen worship there. Everyone was so friendly.

Mrs. Hogue said I would have to see their market before I left Taiwan. There is a large one under cover and many out on the street. The large one was quite a sight. You could buy almost anything there. They have little refrigeration so they must butcher daily, but one is sure of fresh meat. Live chickens are in cages by the counters and live fish are swimming around in tubs. The customer can pick out the fish or chicken she wants and it is slaughtered at once and dressed in a few minutes. I saw one poor old rooster get his last rites and that was enough—I moved on. It was a gruesome place. Chicken heads and feet are eaten in soup and are considered a delicacy. I saw a lot of intestines hanging on a board but was afraid to ask how they were used.

Vegetables of all kinds were on display. They looked so fresh and good. Mrs. Hogue bought ten lovely roses for about 38¢ in our money. Dishes were spread out on the ground at one stand and clothing for sale was spread out on a sheet or rack. Such a jostling there was—just like sidewalk days back home.

I was amused by the musical garbage trucks in Taipei. They have free pickup every day but the people do not put the garbage out in cans and bags as we do. A musical recording of "The Maiden's Prayer" blares out all over the place to alert people to get their garbage ready. Then they come from every direction with some kind of container and each one dumps his own garbage in the truck. No one seemed to know why this particular piece of music was chosen. I was at prayer meeting one evening and everyone was on their knees praying when the garbage truck came by blaring away so loudly I forgot what I was praying about.

A touching incident happened shortly after I went to Taipei. Pastor Yang came up to get Mr. Youeh to have him interpret for some GIs who were going to build a boy's dormitory at the Home. He brought with him a boy from the Home who had won three medals in an athletic meet. My last night at the Home I asked to take his picture but he had gone into town. He so badly wanted to have a picture taken of him and me together that he was willing to travel the fifteen-hour round trip for it. I sent him one of the pictures of us and the Home had an enlargement made from it. He cherished it highly. It must have meant so much to that poor fifteen-year-old boy to have someone from another country interested in his accomplishments. What heartaches these dear orphans must have who do not have anyone to care for them in a special way!

When the day came to say a final goodbye to Taiwan, I was touched by all the wonderful people who came to see me off. Mrs. Yang, and even Jack Hu who had the Christian book store in Kaohsiung, made the long trip—almost a day's ride. Before going to the airport Mrs. Yang Shu brought me a large piece of white paper which had many Chinese characters beautifully drawn on it. She said that "a friend of a friend" knew the last living heir of the famous Chinese philosopher, Confucius. He was the seventy-seventh generation heir. Pastor and Mrs. Yang's friends had told him about my visit to Taiwan and their Home, and something of my work for orphans and asked him to make a wall hanging of one of Confucius' sayings for me. They reported that upon hearing of my work, he was glad to do so.

Jean Chang mounted the scroll for me as the Chinese do and sent it to me by mail later. She translated the scroll to read:

> What has conferred is called the Nature; an accordance with this nature is called The Path of Duty; the regulation of the path is called Instruction.
> The path may not be left for an instant. If it could be left, it would not be the path.

"Good grief," as Charlie Brown would say—to have something made especially for me by a member of the Confucius clan! I think it is the most unusual gift I have ever received.

CHAPTER 12

How God Has Provided

God never gives us a job to do without making conditions possible for us to do it. It has been wonderful how he has provided for this work—many times in ways I have never dreamed.

This project has been a personal one and is in no way connected with any church or institution. I am not wealthy, living on small retirement incomes, so provision for this work had to come from God.

When I first began this work I was teaching, and used of my salary and profits from hand-loomed articles sold for gifts to finance expenses. After I made the trip to Korea, and subsequent trips, I was asked many times to speak to various groups about my work and travel experiences. As a result many individuals and groups gave gifts of materials and money to buy other materials and pay for transportation costs for finished clothing. I never used this money to support my orphans or for other religious contributions. Seldom has this fund been completely exhausted.

I watch for sales so the money will provide as much as possible. I seldom send used clothing now as it costs as much to send that kind as new. With increased rates, I want the money to provide as much wear as possible. Speaking engagements have taken so much of my time that weaving has had to be greatly curtailed.

During the early years of this work, I sent over 1,000 yards of material to the orphanages, as some of the superintendents had said they would make it up into clothing. Prices were much lower then. A lady in Ohio is doing the same type of work and has sent me boxes of yard goods and some finished garments, which I deeply appreciated. Another elderly lady sent beautiful crocheted scarves. The girls—and even the boys—loved them. I am now limiting what I send to only what I can make, due to the high shipping costs.

Mrs. Bae made up many yards of cloth, which I sent her, into clothing for children of lepers.

I have several large boxes of patterns for both

boys' and girls' clothing from infant to size 14 of various styles. Most of the patterns were discontinued by stores and were given to me; others came from individuals.

I try not to send two or more alike garments to the same orphanage. If several dresses are cut over the same pattern, I use different materials and trim them in various ways so each child has an individual look, which they love. Superintendents have written about how delighted the children are with the dresses I make because there is such a variety and the children do not all look alike as is generally the case with orphanages.

The English sign in Taiwan reads: "The clothing of these children are given by Miss Eveline Ritchie. They put them on with thanksgiving to her. Christian Mountain Children's Home."

Sometimes I will cut out garments for several weeks at a time. I have boxes for each size and many times I have several boxes full of cut material before I begin sewing. I like to do the cutting-out in the summer when I can have the clutter in my studio and not scattered over the house.

Nearly all of the sewing is done in the fall and winter in my dining room, as my studio is not heated in the winter. For trimming I use bias tape, ricrac braid, bits of lace and ribbon, decorative machine stitching, and contrasting materials. I seldom use material that is not washable.

I am asked many times how long it takes to make a garment. That is a question which is difficult to answer as I seldom finish a garment as I go. Patterns differ as to style, and some make up faster than others. To save time in changing thread color and attachments on my machine, I do as much on as many different garments as I can with each change. I will do all the zigzagging over the seams of as many garments of one color as possible. I feel the zigzagging will be more substantial than pinking the seams. Hems of many garments, zippers, buttonholes and buttons are done in groups. One day I made over 100 buttonholes. When the stitch is set for gathering, I do many sleeve tops or gather waistlines. I find I save time by doing it this way.

My aim has been to ship out the boxes of finished garments not later than early in April. I have a good friend who takes orders for Avon products and supplies me with the strong boxes in which these orders are shipped.

So many nice scraps are left after cutting out the garments and are too large to throw away, so I piece them up for children's comforters. It would take too long to quilt them so I knot or tie the top, filling, and back together.

To avoid monotony in piecing hit-and-miss whatever comes along, I am making a book of original designs to see how many kinds of patterns I can create from a simple 4½ inch square and four small squares which, when sewn together, make a square the size of the large one. It is amazing how many beautiful effects can be made from these simple patterns, depending on the arrangement of colors and stripe directions. I am trying some interesting ideas with simple rectangular blocks, any size one wants to use. I work out the designs first on squared paper with colored crayons. This way I can determine how many of each kind of block to cut out.

For filling I use old blankets not too badly worn, washable drapes and curtains of medium weight, and smooth bedspreads which are colorfast and with no tufting. The nicest linings are made of one piece of material, although I often piece the backing with large size blocks.

In my "spare time," I knit caps, scarves, hoods, and head warmers. I have made over 400 of them in all colors, combinations, and a variety of patterns. I generally work at this while listening to some favorite programs on our Christian radio.

I am sure God has given me the desire to do this work. I have been doing it since 1956 and am just as eager to get at my sewing today as when I started. I have made more than 3700 garments of all kinds and over 200 comforters. I always put the boxes in His care when I send them out and God has wonderfully taken care of them in transit to far-off countries. I do not know of one that has failed to reach its destination. I think the fact that they do get through has helped to keep up my interest in continuing this work.

Many designs for comforters can be made from a 4½-inch square and four small squares.

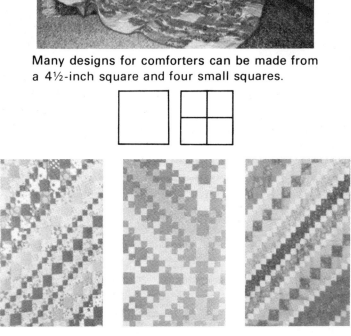

149

In my "spare time" I have knit more than 400 caps, scarves, hoods and head warmers for the orphans.

I have received so many pictures of children wearing the clothing I have made, which is proof they did get it. What a thrill it is to bring happiness to the heart of a little unfortunate child who has seen more sorrow and poverty than many of us will ever know. The children in these Homes receive Bible training and are taken to church. It is amazing the amount of Scripture they memorize. One boy memorized the entire book of Matthew. They learn to pray, and in almost every letter I have from the orphans they tell me how they pray for me.

We do not know the potential for the future for each child we save from a life of abject poverty, despair and often debauchery. All we can do is give them a chance to grow physically, morally, and spiritually, able to take their place in the world as responsible citizens. Who knows, a world figure may come from one of these Homes who will be God's man of the hour in a time of crisis. Each life saved, either great or small, is an asset to the world.

I have been encouraged many times by the story of Dorcas in the book of Acts in the New Testament. God thought it was of enough importance to have it recorded for all time in His Word. There must have been so few engaged in her unique ministry that God considered it necessary to raise her from the dead. I have wondered how she felt about being raised from the dead and able to go back to her old job.

I have always felt that the distribution of the gospel and supplying physical needs when necessity requires it should go hand in hand, and those are the types of organizations I am helping. Many souls have been won to the Lord because someone cared enough about their physical needs to lend a helping hand. It is Christian love in action and this helps them to better understand God's love for them.

I can't think of any class of people who are more deserving of help than little orphans. They didn't ask to come into this old world. The suffering so many have to endure is almost beyond belief. Those who are homeless wherever they can find a bit of shelter, resort to garbage dumps for food and depend on old rags for clothing. I have learned that 5 million children die from starvation each year in India. In some places their little bodies are shoveled up in trucks and taken away and burned. In other places mothers sell their children for $5 apiece, because they can no longer feed them. Others are taken to large cities and deliberately lost because of dire poverty in their homes.

It is no wonder their little hearts almost burst with joy when someone cares enough to be their sponsor. It is a small thing to do to bring so much happiness now and such great potential for the future. To know someone cares what happens to them gives them a desire to amount to something when they grow up. Mine have often told me they will study hard to make me proud of them. Words cannot express the joy I have received from doing what I could for these precious children.

If you should feel you have no one who cares for you and you are of no more use in the world, just take an orphan or two to sponsor and life will change for both of you. These children almost worship a sponsor. It is a wonderful family project to have the children help with the support and planning for the orphan. How thrilled the orphan child is to have a family caring for him or her! I read a letter from a seventy-year-old man who had been sponsoring one. He said if people only knew the joy there was in doing this, there wouldn't be enough children to go around. I can say a hearty "Amen" to that.

The Bible says, "He that hath pity upon the poor lendeth unto the Lord; and that which he hath given will he repay him again" (Proverbs 19:17). What a multitude of ways God has of repaying us! This story would not be complete without recording some of the ways God has provided for my personal needs since I have been occupied in this work. He has promised to take care of our needs if we seek first His kingdom and His righteousness (Matthew 6:33). I have been deeply impressed at how many times God uses other human beings to supply our needs. He could take care of any need we could possibly have all alone, but He doesn't work that way as a rule. He has blessings He wants to bestow on us because of our concern for others going through some difficulty.

A very special need was filled when I bought my last car. During the summer of 1974 I was considering trading off my old car for a good used one. I had talked to one of the deacons at my church about it and he said he would be on the lookout for one. I took my old car to a service station one day and was informed that the exhaust system was so rusted it could go to pieces anytime.

I was petrified at the thought of going to a used car lot and trying to pick out one as I know so little about the inside workings of a car. About all I know about a car is how it looks on the outside and whether it runs or not. I called this deacon and told him the problem I had and he said he would see if he could find a car for me.

Several weeks before this, we had had a lesson in our weekly prayer meeting about asking God definitely for what we wanted. Not just in generalities but in specifics. I decided to put this thought to the test and ask Him for just the kind of car I wanted. These were my specifications: a small car, low mileage, good gas mileage, good condition, not over two years old, light color (not flashy), and not over $1,000 in price. I certainly prayed that evening.

About 9 o'clock the next morning the phone rang and my deacon friend said he thought he had a car for me and would drive it over about noon to see if I liked it. I think I was about as incredulous as the early Christians were when they were praying for the release of the Apostle Peter and he was suddenly standing at the gate. It didn't seem possible an answer could come so soon, less than a day from the time I learned about the condition of my car.

The deacon had seen an ad in the evening paper and had checked it out. My curiosity almost got me down before he came, wondering what kind of a car was to be the answer to my prayer.

When the car finally came, it was small all right— a little Honda 600 sedan. It was so small it was actually cute. The mileage—under 14,000 miles. Gas mileage averaged 35 miles to the gallon. Condition— very good; it looked almost like new. Age—two years old. Color—light yellow, which I like. And the price— $1,000. Exactly what I had asked for!

God also added some goodies which I hadn't asked for, such as: a radio, seat belts, good tires, rust-proofing and front wheel drive. God has promised to "do exceeding abundantly above all we ask or think" (Ephesians 3:20).

The deal was quickly closed. How I did appreciate the kindness and helpfulness of this man. He took the car back to his home and he and his son washed and waxed it until it looked like a brand-new car.

I think the angels must have smiled as they watched the little car dashing down the highway to its new owner and home with its makeup on and all shined up. It has been a joy to drive. It is just the right size for a little old lady to putter around town in, for that is about all the driving I do anymore.

It has its off days, as all cars do, but there has always been someone to lend me a helping hand.

My little Honda is just the right size for a little old lady to putter around town in.

When we need help, God always knows just who to send to give assistance. How closely we should live to the Lord—for we never know when He is going to tap us to help someone solve a problem.

Another outstanding example of God's concern for our needs was a leaky roof over an enclosed porch just off my kitchen. I had just had two enclosed porches reroofed and hoped the problem had been solved, but it wasn't. It was thought the trouble was coming from the kitchen roof. I didn't feel I could afford another big roofing bill so soon.

TAKING OUT MY BUCKETFUL

One Sunday afternoon a new young couple in our church came to call on me. They had learned that the young man's grandmother and I had been special friends during my junior year in high school. Due to this long-ago contact, they wanted to get acquainted with me.

During the conversation I was telling them about my roof problem. He said he would fix it for me. I was very much surprised at such a generous offer the first time we had met. He said that if I provided the material, he would get someone at the church to help him and they would put a new roof on the kitchen. He came one evening to measure the roof for materials and noticed the roof over one bedroom was in a bad condition and offered to do that also.

An evening was set to begin work. Not two men came, but nine! They almost finished the two roofs in that one evening. Several days later, five men came back and finished the job.

I wanted to provide a meal for the men after they quit work but they wouldn't let me. Several women from the church came later with well-filled baskets and we had a regular picnic meal. What a tremendous lift all of this was. I shall never forget it.

God has such strange ways of working out His plans. Sixty years before this He let me become acquainted with a girl who would in the distant future have a kindhearted grandson—who would get acquainted with me at just the time I needed the help he could give. How is that for long-range planning? He knew there would be kindhearted people here at the right time to help this young man. Some people will say it just happened. I don't think anything "just happens" to Christians. How little I dreamed back in those long-ago school days what it would mean to me someday to have been a friend to Marjorie.

I have read the verses of Psalms 41:1-3 many times and wondered if I had met the conditions sufficiently to claim this promise if I became very ill:

Blessed is he that considereth the poor:
   the Lord will deliver him in time of trouble.
The Lord will preserve him, and keep him alive,
   and he shall be blessed upon the earth;
and thou wilt not deliver him unto the will of his
   enemies.
The Lord will strengthen him upon the bed of
   languishing:
Thou wilt make all his bed in his sickness.

How does God make one's bed in sickness? I had a chance to find the answer in the spring of 1976.

I learned through X rays that I had gall bladder trouble. I had never had an attack to make me suspicious of this. I was told it could flare up at any time. I felt that since I knew of the condition, if I had serious trouble, I would have no one to blame but myself if I hadn't done anything about it. I was convinced God had alerted me to my condition. As soon as arrangements could be made, I had it removed. I had a wonderful surgeon, good nursing care, and came through the ordeal so fast it surprised everyone. I was driving my car ten days after the operation.

It was worth the discomfort of surgery to learn how many real friends I had during that time. I live alone and my nearest relatives are hundreds of miles away. My only brother lives in Missouri so none of my relations could be with me during that time. It was wonderful to see how many friends rallied to my support.

My pastor and two kind ladies from my Sunday School class were with me that morning before surgery—and the ladies stayed until I was conscious again. All three came nearly every day I was in the hospital, as well as many other friends. Still others showed their thoughtfulness in other ways. When I came home, ladies from the church saw that I had a complete hot meal for eight days. Everything was so deeply appreciated. God certainly knows how to "make a bed in sickness."

These three instances were major problems that I couldn't solve myself, so God took over and wonderfully helped. There have been many others. Is God concerned with the many small, day-to-day difficulties that plague all of us? Some people say we shouldn't bother God with little things. When He told us to bring our problems and burdens to Him, He never specified the size they had to be before He would be interested. Anything that is of concern to us is important in His sight.

A relatively small incident has happened twice as as I have sent three large boxes of clothing away. They were quite heavy and I asked God to help me get a place to park close to the door at the Post Office, so I wouldn't have to carry them far. As I drove past the building all places were taken near the door. Just as my car entered the entrance to the parking lot, a car backed away from right in front of the door. How I did thank Him. The times are legion when He has worked out difficulties.

A kind neighbor family has helped me so often

Packages
of clothing are
ready to mail.

with property problems I couldn't handle. I praise God for them.

As I have been recalling the events in this writing, I have been amazed all over again at the many things God has done through these years. I am so glad He can use us common garden variety petunias as well as the rare orchids in His work. We never get too old to be in His employ. His retirement plan is out of this world. It seems, though, that the recognition I have received is all out of proportion to what I have done.

I was named the Senior Citizen of the Year for Midland County in 1965 and Senior Citizen of the Year for Service for the State of Michigan the same year. My story was published in *Power For Living* Sunday School paper by Scripture Press. There were the stories of my trip to Taiwan in the three largest newspapers there. Several articles have also appeared in our local newspaper. What a surprise all of this was! I have only tried to do my part.

There are so many worthwhile things that we retirees can do that no one needs to be without a job. Many services do not cost anything in money. Our salvation is a free gift from God, if we will just receive it through Jesus Christ, but our rewards in Heaven depend on our work for Him here.

When I try to compare what I had planned to do for these last years with what God has done for me, it makes me tremble to think of what I would have missed had I not let Him direct my life. The wonderful friendships with people of other lands, the opportunity of meeting so many of them on those three tremendous trips which took me into eighteen countries and provided so many unusual experiences that have enriched my life and memories. The many opportunities for service to those in desperate need. The joy and satisfaction of feeling needed and the chances to give encouragement to the discouraged and point them to the only One who can really help. All these bring a happiness this world cannot give.

It hardly seems true yet that all of these things—and many more—actually happened to me. Life has been anything but boring.

I never know what will happen next.